AUSTRALIA

According to
Hoges

We're not PERFECT but we're WORKING ON IT!

AUSTRALIA
According to
Hoges

We're not PERFECT but we're WORKING ON IT!

PAUL HOGAN

with Tony Davis & Dean Murphy

HarperCollins*Publishers*

To three Aussie greats: John Cornell,
Olivia Newton-John and David Gulpilil.
Much of this book celebrates what it means
to come from 'the land down under',
and no one reflected these qualities better
than these true friends and colleagues.

Contents

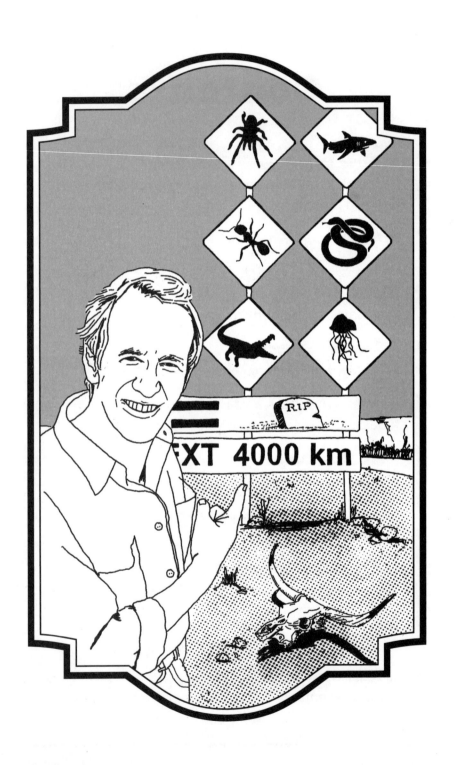

It Could Only Happen Down Under

Welcome to my little wander through Australia, past and present

This might come as a surprise, but I've been around for quite a while now. In fact, I've just clocked up eighty-three years. A lot's happened in this country over that time. Only 234 years have passed since the First Fleet deposited Britain's 'rubbish' on these shores, and I've been around for more than a third of that time. See what I mean by 'quite a while'?

I held the hand of my grandmother when I was a little kid. Later I would reflect on how her hand once held onto the hand of her grandfather, who was born back in convict times. Back then, there wasn't even a country called Australia.

I came into the world right at the start of World War II – might have even caused it – and even that all seems like ancient history. We had a bomb shelter in the backyard. It was just a ditch with a sheet of galvanised iron over the top that appeared to do little other than provide housing for several families of daddy-long-legs spiders and the odd mouse. Mind you, I'm sure we would have enthusiastically dived in there if Japanese planes had suddenly appeared overhead.

I remember the sirens. I remember the blackouts, the dark blinds on all the windows, being told to be scared of the 'evil' Japanese. Not that I ever remember actually being scared. My sister and brother and me, we were just tiny kids, and little people never think of the danger. I thought at the time it was sort of cool that we had a bomb shelter. We probably would have thought it exciting if the Japanese had bombed the Western Suburbs of Sydney, where we lived.

Witnessing history

There's very few of us left from the time when Japan tried to obliterate Darwin. Back then the 'Japs' were despised, and that lingered long after the war finished. The First Nations people – the true Original Australians – weren't even counted as people, and there were all sorts of names for those who came from overseas, looked a bit different or behaved differently.

Australians were always the first to stick up their hands when anyone mentioned there was a war on, so we were recognised around the world as soldiers, and not much else. Perhaps because of our humble beginnings, I think we had a desperation to be known as something more than good soldiers, and over time it has happened.

I have been a first-hand witness to so much of it: the postwar recovery, when we learnt to build things like the first Holden car and the Snowy Mountains hydro-electric scheme; the sporting successes from the 1956 Olympics onwards that

When I was young he seemed so much taller, but here's champion runner Ron Clarke standing on a fruit box so he can light the Olympic flame at the 1956 games in Melbourne. Australia would be changed forever.

started to define us as a sporting nation; the rise of the teenager; the establishment of television and movie industries, which allowed us to tell our own stories; the burgeoning of the arts, science and technology; and the overdue respect for nature and our unique flora and fauna. I have seen our attitudes to foreign people, cultures and languages, and our treatment of Australia's First Nations people turn 180 degrees.

Back in the 1980s there was a bloke with blond hair and blue eyes who did some tourism commercials promoting Australia to the rest of the world. For quite a while that's how many people in other countries thought all Australians looked. There's certainly a group of people who still look like that, but

I donned some of Ms Liberty's clobber for one of our 1980s tourism ads and stood on top of the Sydney Harbour Bridge. The things a bloke will do to sell Oz to the Yanks.

our makeup is now so much more varied, so much richer. I don't think it's an exaggeration to say that Australia has become the most diverse nation on earth, and perhaps the most tolerant. It's full of great people from every corner of the globe. As I've said many times: *What makes a great Australian? Wanting to be one.*

The view from there and here

Yes, I've lived in the US since 2006, to spend as much time as possible with my youngest son, Chance. But if you put a kangaroo in the zoo in San Diego, it's still a kangaroo. An Australian at the top of Kings Canyon is the same person on top of the Empire State Building. Being Australian travels with us. It's so much more than where we pay our phone bill.

And – this is the really important bit – when you live for a little while in another country and come back here, it hits you, every single time: this is a pretty good place. I've returned for a few weeks or months almost every year to spend time with the rest of my family in New South Wales and Queensland, and to enjoy all the great things right across the rest of this amazing country. I've watched its rapid development, and I've thought a lot about what makes Australia what it is, and what makes Australians what they are today. And I've reflected on how pleased I am that our country has changed in the ways it has, rather than in all the other ways it could have. It has improved.

On our way

So here is *Australia, According to Hoges*. It's not a history of our country, so much as my thoughts on some of that history, and it's not a history of me, though I've included some yarns from my ridiculously lucky and colourful life where they help illustrate the bigger picture. For those who really do want a history of me, which is to say my stellar career working on the Sydney Harbour Bridge and my slight diversions into television and movies, my occasional brushes with Hollywood royalty and actual royalty, and reflections on a marriage or two, check out my other book, *The Tap-Dancing Knife Thrower*.

This book is about the country that has given me so much. I've lived what they call the American Dream, where you go from being a genuine blue-collar worker with nothing to a huge success, but I've done it in Australia, which is even better. It truly is a land of opportunity.

I love this country with its red soil and white beaches. I love its people's unique sense of humour, can-do spirit and mischievous nature (what we call larrikinism). But, most of all, I love this country's sense of fairness. We're not perfect – not yet – but we're working on it.

I hope you have fun joining me on this little trip through the past and into the present.

PH, October 2022

PS: For those unfamiliar with our Aussie brand of English, I've also included pointers on how to speak ''Strayan', with definitions of some favourite local expressions throughout these pages and in Chapter 4. Hopefully, by the time you've read the book, you'll be speaking and understanding 'Strayan like a local.

yarn

A *yarn* is a story, and we admire people in this country who can tell a good one. It probably goes back to long nights around the campfire in the middle of nowhere. If someone is *telling* a yarn, it could be true, or it could be slightly embellished, but the important thing is that it is entertaining. If someone's *spinning* a yarn, then they're making it up, and probably for all the wrong reasons. Strangely, newspaper journalists call their stories yarns, and they are supposed to be true. When I had a television show and we had skits and singing and even dancing (thank you, Maria), many people still thought the best part was the simplest: when I just sat down and told a yarn straight to camera. Why? Probably because it was relatable. I'd like to say that the art of telling a yarn is a skill I learnt at work and at the pub from a whole lot of other good talkers. But I can't because I didn't learn anything when I was young, as I just didn't listen. I was the one always yakking on, the one that had all the opinions and ideas. Being a chatterbox came naturally, and it was fine when I was working on the Bridge and really did think I knew everything. When I got on television I had to start listening. I had to comment on things that were happening in the wider world, and you couldn't do that unless you shut your mouth and opened your ears. I learnt then not to be the know-all. One time, my mate and business partner John 'Corny' Cornell and I were sitting in a bar somewhere and we'd had a few drinks and he congratulated me on not getting a big head when I started turning up on television screens. And I said, quite honestly, 'Mate, I had one before I started turning up on the TV. You made me pull my head in, at least a little.'

CHAPTER 1

Originals and Blow-ins

Meet the residents

Years ago, when I was fronting television commercials for the Australian Tourism Commission, I argued that we shouldn't be advertising the landscape – or, as I put it, 'the furniture' – because almost every country has waterfalls and a beach or two that they can dress up for the cameras. What we should be advertising, I said, was the people, because it's the people that make a place worth visiting.

It's taken us many years, some resilient original occupants, and several waves of incomers, or blow-ins, as we say, to give this country its modern makeup. Yet amazingly, we are now, in my view, the friendliest, most welcoming bunch in the world. There's more than 200 different nationalities living here, getting on remarkably well, and wanting to be part of this Australian adventure. If we take a quick look at our dodgy past, you'll see what an unlikely success story that is.

Let's hear it for the Originals

As far as most of the world was concerned, our continent didn't exist until the Dutch spotted us, or tiny bits of our coastline, a few hundred years ago. But it did exist, and people had been living here for 60,000 years or more. They were the Originals.

Different people have different ideas as to whether the Originals walked here or boated here, but the general belief is that they came out of Africa then travelled over various landmasses before crossing into Australia from New Guinea via a land bridge. When the water levels rose, the Originals found themselves on their own separated continent.

These first arrivals, or First Nations as they are now known, tended to live in small groups. They weren't united and the groups seldom came in contact with other groups, or mobs, as they say, because they were scattered across this great continent. Yet they still developed along similar lines. They had the same sort of culture and the same sort of beliefs. Their driving force was survival. What they wanted out of life, from what I've seen of their culture, was to live and let live, and be happy.

Despite the size of the country, the different First Nations groups must have communicated with each other, because almost every mob shared a belief in the Dreamtime or Dreaming, which is the Originals' version of the creation story, the spirit world and the afterlife combined. They depicted some of the stories of the Dreamtime in their art, which always had a purpose. They didn't just write 'Fred was here.' They passed on messages and their thoughts and what happened. What was sacred and what wasn't.

They lived off the earth and survived in a place that can

be incredibly dry and hostile. In recent years, some farmers and graziers have been returning to the lessons the Originals learnt over 60,000 years of Indigenous life in dealing with water and land management.

Bushfires are something we consider as inescapably Australian as sharks. But the Originals used to light fires deliberately. They understood that you needed to get rid of all the dead scrub, the underlying branches, for the trees to regenerate. As a result, the land flourished, and they never had a real bushfire problem. If only we'd been that smart.

The First Nations people were the original storytellers, the original entertainers, educating their children and passing on their history through great yarns and dance and music and art. In recent times, even the most cynical people have started to acknowledge the importance of art and music to the health and success of every culture.

The Originals had a great respect for their Elders, and the wisdom they would impart. While I now like to consider myself an elder of my own tribe (because I've been around for so long), I'm not sure too many people listen to me. And, sadly, I have to admit I never listened to my elders when I was young. Should have of course, but me and my mates were sure we were smarter than they were.

One of the big things the Originals achieved as they developed independently, from what I've seen, is a lack of greed. And greed's the great driver of all other wanting: wanting other people's property and, ultimately, other people's territory.

A lot of people don't realise how important laughter is to the Originals. Some of that we picked up, and it may be one of the reasons why today's Australians are so laid-back.

Grand designs

It's believed there were hundreds of thousands of the original occupants here when the first ship arrived from Europe. (I like to say *occupants* rather than *owners* because the planet's been here for billions of years and we're all ants crawling on it for just a few seconds. Five minutes, maybe, but then we're gone.) And they'd been living here for tens of thousands of years before Europeans realised the continent even existed.

The Europeans were too stupid to realise they could learn a lot from the Originals. Something that has always impressed me, for example, is that hundreds, possibly thousands of years before anyone else, the Originals discovered aerodynamics and understood physics. The great demonstration of that, I think is the woomera, which was the rocket launcher of its time. The Romans had spears two thousand years ago, but the only people who worked out a way to make them fly further and harder and quicker were the Australian Originals.

One little guy probably saw that big guys had an unfair advantage. Even if they weren't physically stronger, the guys with the longest arms could throw further. Then that little guy realised if he could make his arms longer, he could hurl the spear further and more forcefully. So he invented the woomera, which is a piece of carefully shaped wood with a notch in the end where you insert the base of a spear. The woomera became an extension of the arm. And that's physics: the geometry, the levers.

The little guy, or one of his mates, probably noticed that the basic throwing spear could be improved too. With a sharp point, you have to hit the creature you're aiming at with an accuracy of a couple of inches. So they invented the waddy, a hunting stick, which, instead of having a point, had more of a blade. This was so that even if small game shifted a few inches at the last minute, you'd still bring it down because your strike area was no longer the size of the point, it was the width of the blade.

It all comes down to physics: the woomera was the rocket launcher of its time.

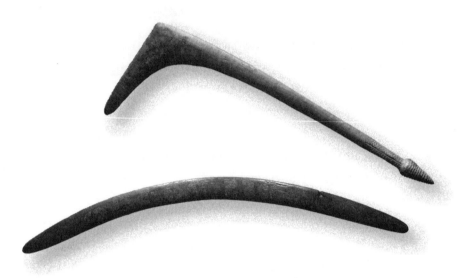

The waddy and boomerang. If only the Wright brothers had taken notice,
they could have invented flying thousands of years earlier!

And that waddy and that blade probably led to the most famous Australian invention of any time, modern or ancient, the boomerang. The Originals might have discovered by accident that when this bent stick was shaped a certain way, it would turn in the air and fly back to the thrower. But, once they did, they learnt they could repeat and refine the design. The boomerang exploited aerodynamics in a way that had never been done anywhere else, hundreds of years before those Wright brothers could get anything to lift off the ground and go in a straight line for even fifty yards.

Another innovation was the bullroarer, a flat, oval piece of wood attached to a long string, which, when spun in the air, created a loud whirring sound the Originals used as a signal. The bullroarer was about aerodynamics too. It's all in the way you shape the wood. I made one for *Crocodile Dundee II*. The trick is to get the piece of wood circling and rotating at the same time. That's where the roar comes from. How they came up with that one, again I don't know, but a bullroarer can make an enormous sound that travels a great distance. Male Originals would send it out to let the other men know that there was a gathering, or corroboree. Women weren't invited, but they had their own meetings and gatherings.

Almost every early culture had a drum of some sort, to beat out rhythms that were probably inspired by the heartbeat. But our Originals had what blow-ins call the digeridoo. (In northern Australia, where it was invented, it's known as a yidaki or mandapul.) It's a wooden wind instrument, the like of which had never been seen anywhere else. It makes this haunting sound, and it's hard not to be moved when you hear it, particularly if it's accompanied by someone tapping out a rhythm on wooden clapsticks.

The purpose of the didge and the sticks was to make music to dance to, whether for entertainment or to teach and pass on stories and knowledge. Entertainer and all-round good bloke Ernie Dingo can play the vacuum-cleaner pipes. A couple of extensions from a Hoover and he's off. And it sounds just great.

How to Speak 'STRAYAN

tucker

Food. *Bush tucker* is the stuff the Originals lived on, and we were too daft, until recently, to pay it any mind. There's a lot of good munga out there in the Never Never.

OUR HOMEGROWN CREATURES

Across this huge nation, we've got numbats, wombats, echidnas, Tasmanian devils, frill-necked and thorny devil lizards, and bloody big goannas, lyrebirds and sugar gliders and quokkas, emus and cassowaries, kookaburras and rosellas, and more marsupials and creatures that hop than the rest of the world put together.

On that last score, kangaroos are famous all around the world. To most people, a kangaroo is cute – shy, with a sweet face. But to a farmer, it's a six-foot rat. Australian farmers cull kangaroos every so often, killing sometimes up to a million a year because they almost outnumber us. And usually they become dog food, even though kangaroo is great meat, really lean and almost fat free.

Kangaroos, or roos, can be dangerous. In times gone by, travelling circuses and fairs put boxing gloves on kangaroos and challenged onlookers to fight them. But this was just a gimmick. The front legs weren't a concern; it was the lower limbs that could do real damage. Roos can be big powerful creatures. When they think they are threatened, they lean back on their tail and strike with their powerful rear legs, dragging them down a foe in a ripping motion. They can tear out your insides, just like that.

At my place up at Byron Bay, we had platypuses in the creek. We'd sneak down and sit there just before sunset, when you'd see them swimming. There were never many, and they are a rare sighting in the wild, so it was amazing to witness. We also had flying foxes, wallabies and, just in one tree, koalas. The platypus is one of the weirdest animals in the world. It looks like it couldn't decide whether it was going to be a duck or an otter. If you decide to pick it up because it looks cute, watch out, because it has a defence mechanism: poisonous spurs on its hind legs.

The who–art snake

Ellen DeGeneres once said Australia might be a great place for a holiday, except everything down there kills you. And she was sort of right. We don't have lions and rhinos like Africa, but from the snakes and spiders on the land to the crocs and sharks and stingers in the water, Australia is out to get you.

We do brag a bit about it. The place with the most great white sharks in the world? South Australia! Crocodiles? Yeah, we're pretty well covered there too – up north is crawling with them. Poisonous spiders, poisonous things in the water? Yep, everything out here bites or stings you. Cobra? Come on, mate, our inland taipan is the most venomous snake in the world. Even our eastern or common brown snake is way out there on the poison front. And they're angry buggers too; I've seen one attack a car. What was he gonna do with it? I don't know. But he was really having a go. You have to admire an animal with that much mongrel in him.

I remembered telling some people in the States that we call the inland taipan the who-art snake. We call it that, I explained, because if one of them bites you and you're religious, you'll start saying 'The Lord's Prayer'. And the fourth word is about as far as you'll get before you're dead: 'Our father who art ...'

A good line in spiders

Okay, we sometimes overstate things. Americans talk about the black widow biting through the hard skin on the palm of your hand. We tell them an angry funnel-web – the most poisonous spider in the world, according to many studies – can bite you through the bottom of an army boot. It can't quite do that, but it can go through the leather on the top of a shoe, which is impressive enough.

One of the reasons Australia wasn't ideal for my former wife Linda is that she's an arachnophobe. You just have to say 'spider' and she gets scared. And this country does a pretty good line in spiders. Her parents came out for our wedding in 1990. They were from upmarket Connecticut and didn't really know anything about Australia. Their image of it was like the wildest parts of Africa, or something along those lines. Our Dundee films probably didn't help.

We put Linda's parents up in a little house on the property. It was the original farm cottage, and when we bought the place we'd originally planned to put a gallon of petrol on it and set fire to it. But a mate suggested he fix it up. Good idea, because it came up nicely.

Anyway, it was up on the hill, in a wonderful spot, completely secluded. And that's what scared Linda's parents. Her father, Stanley, asked if they needed a gun. He was quite serious. I don't know if he thought marauders were going to attack, or crocodiles were going to come crawling up from the creek, but he kept saying it: 'If we're going to stay up here, I'd be happier with a gun.'

How to Speak 'STRAYAN

kangaroos loose in the top paddock

If someone's got *kangaroos loose in the top paddock*, they're not all there, not the full quid. They're a dope, a drongo. There are many variations, like *a couple of tins short of a six pack* and *a few sangas (sandwiches) short of a picnic*.

Some pretty ordinary explorers

As I mentioned at the start, when I held my grandmother's hand, I was only one person removed from the convict days, and she once held the hand of her grandfather, who couldn't call himself an Australian. He was a convicted British criminal and had been transported to New South Wales. He couldn't call himself an Australian because there was no such place with that name. It didn't yet exist. It was called New Holland, or Terra Australis (Southern Land), and not long before that it didn't even have those names. Despite 60,000 years of rich culture, it wasn't even on the map as far as the rest of the world was concerned.

When I learnt history at school in the 1940s and 1950s, we were told the Romans, the Etruscans, the Egyptians and others had all been around for thousands of years, but somehow this Great Southern Land didn't seem to exist. Europeans thought if you sailed this far, you'd fall off the edge of the world.

Australians love to learn about other countries and travel to see the ancient pyramids, the Colosseum in Rome, where Russell Crowe used to fight, and all that, but we're usually less

Captain Willem Janszoon, whose maps of our coast were such a mess he may as well have stayed at home in Holland and done them there. Maybe he did.

knowledgeable about our own history, despite it being sixty millennia in the making. When European settlement finally occurred, it was just yesterday in the grand time scale.

The first Europeans to sight this continent were a batch of crazy Dutchmen who sailed down here in the 1600s. Number one, as far as we know, was Captain Willem Janszoon, in his ship *Duyfken* (*Little Dove*), who visited the north coast in 1606. He wasn't sure what he'd found, or whether he was in Australia or the bottom part of New Guinea, or if the two places were connected. He later claimed that ten of his crew were killed by hostile natives, among them some Originals who attacked his sailors with bows and arrows. That's a bit of a clue that Janszoon wasn't too sure which landmass he was on. And for all that, the bloke's maps were unreadable.

The next crazy Dutchman to pay a visit was Dirk Hartog. He always fascinated me: he sailed east from southern Africa across the Indian Ocean, missed his left turn towards the Dutch East Indies and ran straight into the west coast of Australia. Dirk landed on what is now called Dirk Hartog Island. He left a plate saying 'Dirk Was Here' then took off, having found nothing of interest. Nothing of interest? Dirk was clearly a bit of a pelican. Then he sailed up the west coast for a couple of hundred kilometres and charted it but never landed, never wanted to have a look inside. So, in the early maps, the western side of the continent was shown as a long, thin sliver. People assumed it was fifty kilometres wide or thereabouts.

Dirk was representing Holland. That little country could have fitted into Australia two hundred times or something, and was barely staying above the water even then. (And, as the modern-day Netherlands, it may end up well below the water if global warming comes to full fruition.) But Dirk was never tempted to claim our continent for Holland, or land on it, or anything.

How to Speak 'STRAYAN

galah

The galah is a very colourful bird and very loud. But it has no brains. A galah will fly into cars and windows. So if you call a bloke a *galah* you're calling him an idiot, and if you call him a *flaming galah*, you're calling him a flaming idiot. Terms such as wombat and pelican can do a similar job.

Anthony van Diemen, the Governor-General of the Dutch East Indies, whose name was bestowed on the island we know as Tasmania by adventurer and crawler Abel Tasman.

A bit later, in 1642, another Dutchman, Abel Tasman, came along, and his efforts were pretty ordinary too. He missed the whole of mainland Australia, swung in late, narrowly avoiding going over the edge of the world, and found himself looking at what we would later know as Tasmania. Didn't see Australia. Just Tasmania.

How he got to Tassie and didn't see, or didn't report seeing, Australia, I don't know. It's not that far away from Tasmania. And it's quite big too.

Tasman called the island he found Van Diemen's Land, in honour of Anthony van Diemen, Governor-General of the Dutch East Indies, who had paid for Tasman's voyage. So Abel T. was a bit of a crawler, naming the place after his boss. In a modern context it's like someone from the media finding an island and calling it Packer Land, or Rupertstan.

THE EXTRA BIT AT
THE BOTTOM

There's a love–hate relationship between the Australian mainland and Tasmania that goes back a long way. Tasmanians resented us mainlanders, quite often because we'd make maps of Australia without showing Tassie. In fact, that was our revenge, because, as I've noted, Dutch explorer Abel Tasman – for reasons of poor eyesight or something – made a big fuss about Tasmania and didn't even notice Australia. So that's the payback: we leave them off the map because they got on the map first, as if the big bit of this country didn't even exist.

Tasmania was eventually named after Abel Tasman, but at first, as I've mentioned, it was called Van Diemen's Land. People in Australia often thought that meant 'Demon's Land', as if it was Britain's version of Devil's Island, that horrible French prison off French Guiana in South America. In reality, it was worse than that.

The mainland sent all its worst criminals there. I mean, we were all pretty bad to start with, and the worst of the worst they sent to Tasmania. So that's saying something!

I've seen the ruins of the prisons down in Tasmania and you can tell they were the most inhumane places imaginable. You wouldn't put animals in those stone-walled boxes; PETA would be all over you. But the authorities considered those prisoners to be bad to the bone.

As with Devil's Island, just being sent to Van Diemen's Land could be close to a death sentence in itself. The forced labour was backbreaking, the punishments were extreme. I've read that people were sentenced to be flogged and then hanged.

They'd get a couple of hundred lashes, which would almost kill them. Then they'd be killed.

They became hard, that early lot of Europeans in Tassie, and they proved that by almost completely wiping out the native population. They even declared war on them. They called it the Black War, and sent in soldiers and civilians in a long line to push the native people as far south as possible, ideally to a small peninsula that could be easily sealed off. They claimed the Originals were savages anyway, and it had to be done to stop raids on settlers' buildings and poaching of their livestock. Essentially they were trying to wipe them off the face of the earth, and they pretty near succeeded. There was even a bounty on Aboriginal heads at one stage.

So it has a very, very tough history to it, Tassie. Yet it is one of the most beautiful places anywhere, and I've always found the people to be the salt of the earth.

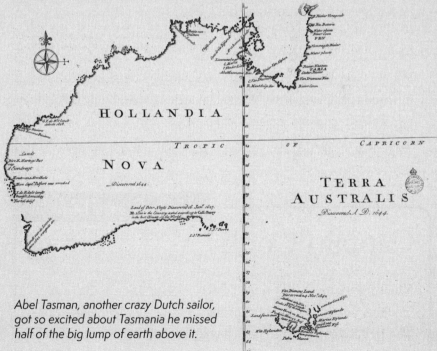

Abel Tasman, another crazy Dutch sailor, got so excited about Tasmania he missed half of the big lump of earth above it.

Cook's tours

For a while that was the entire known map of Australia: a guess at what some of the top bit looked like, outlines of parts of the west coast, with a small island or two thrown in, and Tassie. Just bits here and there, and the whole big continent still didn't exist as far as Europe was concerned. It stayed that way till Jimmy Cook got down here and mapped the east coast nearly up to Queensland. When he did his first Pacific tour (1768–71, followed by comeback tours in 1772–75 and 1776–79), he swung down from Tahiti to New Zealand to have a look, and anchored off a bay there. I reckon about fifty huge Maori probably came out with tattooed faces and started doing the haka, and Cook said, 'Bugger this,' then swiftly pulled up the anchor and sailed away. No doubt he thought, 'There's gotta be somewhere better than this.'

So he sailed across to Australia, and said, 'This'll do.' Why he called it New South Wales, I don't know. I've been to South Wales. You don't take your swimming costume and beach umbrella to Old South Wales. It's not exactly Bondi. Anyway, the British prisons were overcrowded and Cook's reports of Botany Bay made politicians realise this faraway joint would

How to Speak 'STRAYAN

Captain Cook

Rhyming slang. A *Captain Cook* is a look: 'Go on, have a Captain Cook.' You might prefer to have a *butcher's* instead. That comes from a butcher's hook.

make a good place to dump all the pickpockets and loaf-of-bread thieves. The first boatloads of convicts arrived in what is now Sydney in 1788.

English mariner Matthew Flinders was the first to sail right the way around Australia, in 1801–03, and prove it was an island. (Flinders even named the landmass Australia, and eventually the name took off.) Only then could all the maps finally be joined up, nearly two hundred years after Willem J.

If there had been a European rush for the Great Southern Land, the continent could have been split up. If the Dutch had decided, 'We'll have a bit of that juicy looking land,' and if the French explorer Lapérouse had done more than just poked around the east coast and instead decided to get a French foothold here, and if the Spanish and Portuguese had settled in various places, deciding they didn't want to be left out, we could have been a dozen countries, like South America.

I reckon we did all right being settled by the British, if only because they gave us their language. We never would have had such a huge number of successful Hollywood actors if our language had been Portuguese or Dutch. Bit lucky there.

Some blow-ins blow in

As one of our finest modern songwriters, Paul Kelly, sang, from small things, big things grow. Australia's modern immigration started with the lowest of the low, and slowly, reluctantly, built up as we realised the wider world just might have something to offer us. At about the same time, the wider world realised we might have something to offer it too. A modern country was born with remarkable speed.

Here come the Brits

The First Fleet was the name given to the ragtag fleet of eleven ships that first brought Britain's discards to Australia. Under the command of Captain Arthur Phillip, it took about 250 days to reach Botany Bay, which turned out to be not nearly as good as it said in the brochures. So they upped sticks and moved north to a more protected harbour with better soil, fresh water and higher real-estate values. And so it was that this rubbishy lot of convicts, sailors and jailers dropped anchor in Sydney Harbour on 26 January 1788. The Originals kept away mostly, just occasionally coming back for a peek and saying to themselves, 'Check out these funny-looking pink people!' They didn't do the Maori thing and frighten the shit out of everyone, not initially at least. If they came too close, the new arrivals shot at 'em or chased them off.

Instead of doing that, our dopey ancestors should have learnt from their culture and taken a few tips on how to live well in this strange new land. My ignorant forebears probably thought the Originals were 'primitive natives', and had no idea they represented the most ancient culture known on the planet. The funny pink people called the Originals 'Aborigines' then 'Aboriginals', but both words now have negative connotations.

Australians have a tendency to shorten long words and lengthen short ones, as many of the 'How to Speak 'Strayan' entries in this book show. But our slang hasn't always been good. We once called First Nations people *abos* and refugees *refos*. Good riddance to both horrible terms; the really, really offensive part of the first one is that it leaves out *original*, which is the most important part of the word.

We descendants of convicts used to pretend to ourselves, especially when I was a kid, that our ancestors had just been unlucky or poor, or that they'd been persecuted because they were unionised or Irish. Some were, but most of them were villains. That was the fact of it: real shifty. Sent out here for various crimes, usually for seven years, fourteen years or life, and many probably deserved it.

After they'd been in prison here a while, they were rented out to the farmers or road builders who treated them as property. Exactly like slaves. That's why we have empathy with the slaves in America, even though most of our slaves were white.

Australia was essentially a prison farm. But eventually, through mail and chat from returning sailors and whatever, the word got back to Old Blighty that it was pretty cool down here: good weather and wide-open spaces. People started to realise you could be grinding away in a factory in Manchester, constantly rained on and freezing your bits off in winter, or you could be sitting on an Aussie beach with the sun on your back and a cool ocean breeze massaging your face. So they started to come down here voluntarily. The first free settlers arrived in January 1793: five men, two women and six children.

My great-great-grandfather on my mum's side of the family didn't have much choice in the matter. He was a forger, sentenced to fourteen years in what was then called the New South Wales Penal Colony. On my dad's side, the Hogan that came down here said he was a blacksmith, but he was apparently being pursued about some missing horses. He claimed to be a free settler, but that probably just meant he hadn't been caught. Most of the convicts and settlers were dodgy in their own ways, and the people sent out to keep watch on them weren't exactly the cream of the crop either. The government didn't go through the army and figure who were the best, most intelligent officers, and then send them to Australia.

That was the way of it with many of our ancestors: dumped down here and scorned.

The rush for gold

When the Victorian Gold Rush was on from 1851, many people from across Australia and overseas scrambled to grab their share. The Chinese arrived in big numbers, or what the

V. R.

NOTICE!!

Recent events at the Mines at Ballaarat render it necessary for all true subjects of the Queen, and all strangers who have received hospitality and protection under Her flag, to assist in preserving

Social Order

AND

Maintaining the Supromacy of the Law.

The question now agitated by the disaffected is not whether an enactment can be amended or ought to be repealed, but whether the Law is, or is not, to be administered in the name of HER MAJESTY. Anarchy and confusion must ensue unless those who cling to the Institutions and the soil of their adopted Country step prominently forward.

His Excellency relies upon the loyalty and sound feeling of the Colonists.

All faithful subjects, and all strangers who have had equal rights extended to them, are therefore called upon to

ENROL THEMSELVES

and be prepared to assemble at such places as may be appointed by the Civic Authorities in Melbourne and Geelong, and by the Magistrates in the several Towns of the Colony.

CHAS. HOTHAM.

BY AUTHORITY: JOHN FERRES, GOVERNMENT PRINTER, MELBOURNE.

When the miners at Ballarat were getting feisty, the Crown responded with a call to arms (and some pretty dodgy spelling). The Eureka Stockade was afoot.

locals thought were big numbers, and they dug their mines and kept going seven days a week, from early in the morning to late at night. Our lot should have applauded their get up and go, but they didn't see it like that.

Australian miners were starting to unionise, and banned the Chinese. They didn't want them, and certainly didn't want them taking the gold away to China. There were some do-gooders around at the time who thought the Chinese should be treated properly, though not enough obviously.

At the other end of the scale, some people were persuaded or even forced to come and work here. From the 1860s, the practice of blackbirding brought hundreds of Pacific Islanders to Australia. They were promised good jobs but often made to work in slave-like conditions, usually in the cane fields up north.

Strangely, it was the White Australia policy of 1901 that stopped this. The government said, in its self-righteousness, 'We're not having this slavery,' but the real reason for the change

How to Speak 'STRAYAN

Banana Benders

People from Queensland. It might be the best term for people from different states. We also have *Crow-eaters* (South Australians), *Sandgropers* (West Australians), *Top-Enders* (people of the Northern Territory) and *Taswegians* (Tasmanians). People from New South Wales call Victorians *Mexicans*, because they are south of the border, and what Victorians often call their northern neighbours shouldn't be repeated.

STATING THE OBVIOUS

In the late 1800s, the continent had six separate self-governing British colonies: New South Wales, Queensland, Victoria, Tasmania, South Australia and Western Australia. In 1901, they agreed to form the Commonwealth of Australia.

Although Federation, as it was known, was a good thing, the names of the states remained a problem. The US has really interesting names for its states, but Australia, nah. We have Queensland, named in honour of the Queen, and New South Wales, which is nothing like South Wales. And then Victoria, named after the same queen as the joint up north.

And then we became even less imaginative. 'Let's call this one South Australia and this one Western Australia,' and, later, 'That territory up north, what about ... let me think ... Northern Territory?' A lot of imagination must have gone into that.

And although Tasmania was eventually named after the guy who found it, it started out as Van Diemen's Land. Even though Mr Van Diemen had nothing to do with it.

was that they didn't want people of colour staying in Australia. Many islanders got shipped back to the Pacific, not necessarily to where they came from, just wherever it was convenient for a ship's captain to drop them off. It was an utter disgrace.

Most of the Chinese who'd come for the gold were forced to leave (or chose to) but some managed to stay, and many of their descendants set up successful businesses. It became almost a requirement of every town in Australia that you had to have a pub, a school and a Chinese restaurant. I can't remember seeing any decent-sized town across this whole country that didn't have a Chinese restaurant. So we forgave them their supposed misdemeanours in mining because we liked their food. As they say, the way to someone's heart is through their stomach.

More blow-ins with good tucker

When the Queen toured Australia in 1954, she got the train to Parramatta. Don't know why Her Majesty had to take public transport, but she did, and all the houses emptied, and everyone we knew walked down to have a look. Our street came to a dead end at the railway line. We waited there for what seemed like hours for the chance to wave at her and Prince Philip as they stood on the little balcony at the back of the slow-moving train making its way through Granville to Parramatta. I assume the Royal couple stopped their journey there, because anywhere outside Parramatta was out in the sticks. That's where the bulk of the Sydney population lived back then, along the main trainline between Central and Parramatta, and huge crowds turned out to wave.

I was a teenager and you might have expected a teenager to be a bit uninterested in royalty. But we had no television

LET 'ER RIP, BORIS

In August 1972 I agreed to help promote Winfield cigarettes on the telly. In a now-famous ad, I sat in front of the Sydney Symphony Orchestra in a dinner suit and talked about the cigarettes. Then I ad-libbed to the orchestra conductor, 'Let 'er rip, Boris, ol' son.' And with that, the orchestra cranked its way through Tchaikovsky's Fifth Symphony, which, hilariously, became better known in Australia as 'the Winfield theme'.

'Boris' was Geza Bachmann, a one-time member of the Budapest Philharmonic Orchestra, who had come to Australia with his family in 1949, one of millions of new Australians who made it to these shores after World War II. This Hungarian musical genius became head of the Australian Opera Orchestra and a regular on ABC radio with his classical trio. Yet another example of an immigrant enriching the joint.

He was a good sport, old Boris, and I'm sure he was as oblivious as me to the fact that advertising cigarettes was a bad thing to be doing. Those were the days when you couldn't see a war movie without the soldiers stopping for a smoke, or a western without the cowboys lighting up. Cigarettes were good for you.

As I said at the time, dressing me up in a dinner suit for those commercials was like 'putting a top hat on a cockroach'. But on the ol' Geza, the fancy clobber just looked right. He was all class.

The Royal couple, the Queen and the Duke of Edinburgh, caught the train like the rest of us when they visited in 1954. Every house in our street emptied so we could wave back and wish them well.

back then, and it was incredibly exciting to see someone famous who wasn't an Australian, particularly someone you'd seen on stamps and coins and notes. We were impressed, too, by how much she looked just like she did on the stamps and coins and notes.

But something was changing dramatically while we were all waving our British flags at Liz and Phil: us blow-ins were getting a whole new class of blow-in. The White Australia Policy was still in force after World War II, but the government obviously started bending the rules a bit because we needed workers for our factories and our farms and our hydro-electric projects. The Snowy Mountains Scheme, particularly, was a pretty amazing national effort, requiring hundreds of new workers, and it helped change the makeup of our country soon after the war ended. From the late 1940s, migration from places other than the British Isles picked up. Until then, we were pretty much Smiths and Joneses and Donahues. We were overwhelmingly white and either Catholic or Protestant. They were the only two religions that you heard about. No Muslims, Hindus, Buddhists or Jews. None that most of us knew about, anyway.

First came the Italians and the Greeks. The Italians mainly arrived in Sydney, while the Greeks more often went to Melbourne. I think it's still the largest Greek city outside Greece. Suddenly we found foreigners in our classes at school, and a few long, hard-to-pronounce names among the Browns and Kellys and Taylors.

At first, and alas, we called them *wogs* and *dagos*. More politely, they were *refos* (for refugees), even though most of them weren't. There was a bit of hostility, can't deny it. But when we discovered they were real good soccer players, suddenly they weren't refos anymore (let alone the worse names). They were Tony and Mario and Christos. They were New Australians.

We're the only country in the world that treated our foreigners like that. We called them 'New Australians', and we started doing that in the 1950s. You never heard them in the US calling their immigrants 'New Americans', or in Britain 'New Brits'. Here, the mingling was done far quicker than almost anywhere else in the world.

I saw the living proof of how rapidly Australia could adapt and develop. Two of my school gang were Italians. Rocky was Assyrian, Eddie was Chinese, and Les was from Thursday Island.

THE IMMIGRANTS WE SHOULD HAVE KEPT OUT

The First Fleet and the rabble that followed weren't content to live in a country with the greatest array of weird and wonderful animals on earth. Oh, no, with their boofheaded logic, they had to bring in a whole lot of new creatures.

The cane toad, for example, was introduced from Hawaii in 1935. Scientists brought them in because they said they would eat the cane beetles that were damaging Queensland sugar plantations. Then they realised cane beetles can fly and cane toads can't. Shit. We started out with 102 of the horrible toads in 1935, and now it's reckoned there are 200 million, and they're on the move south and west. In various parts of Queensland I've come out of my room at night and they've been everywhere. Ugly as sin, and noisy – and hundreds of the bloody things heading in every direction. They breed like rabbits.

And we all know the other thing that breeds like rabbits. Yeah, rabbits. In 1859, one of our dopey ancestors, Thomas Austin, thought, *Let's bring some of them out here and release them into the wild.* What could go wrong? Only that they reproduced like crazy and soon millions of them

were working their way across the continent, stuffing up crops and grazing lands. We tried to get rid of them by infecting them with the virus that causes the disease myxomatosis. That strategy was initially successful, but then the rabbits started developing resistance to the virus. Now you see them even in cities, though apparently there's a new bug slowing them up a bit.

Back to nature

We've had plenty of other infestations here. Once, I was in the Northern Territory, filming in this swamp. Suddenly, these brumbies, or wild horses, just bolted through. And there were feral camels there too, because from about 1840 we brought them in to cart stuff over our huge expanses of desert. We brought Afghan people too, to run the camel trains. But when the railways and trucks came, the camels were simply released into the wild. There are more than a million of them out there now.

There are also huge numbers of wild pigs and water buffaloes running around in the Top End. Razorback feral pigs are notoriously ugly and have anger-management issues. They are not cute little things like Babe, but huge, scary creatures. They can even kill sheep and eat them. You don't want to get in their way.

While we were bringing in animals that didn't belong, we were eliminating the ones that did. The Tasmanian tiger, for example. Such a fascinating creature, so of course we got rid of it. Apparently better to do that than risk them killing a sheep or a cow. Tragic. In early 2022, the koala – yes, even our cuddly little koala – was added to the endangered species list.

Les was best man at my wedding. I was best man at his too. He called himself Black Les and we didn't think much about it. They were your mates, but they came from all over the planet.

By the time I was in my early teens I'd started to lose that feeling that anyone who wasn't a Smith or a Jones or a Donahue couldn't be an Australian. But I have to admit some resentment always lingered, usually directed at the most recent arrivals. So our Western Suburbs gang, mixed though it was, bad-mouthed the Lebanese because they were starting to arrive in the country in big numbers, particularly out there in Western Sydney.

But suddenly, people like me who had been brought up on British cuisine, realised, 'Hey, Italian tucker's pretty good, isn't it?' Chinese too. Our whole attitude changed. We thanked God they'd come and we no longer had to eat silverside and sausages and two veg every weekend.

The Lebanese brought kebabs, and proved damn good at sport too. Pretty soon they weren't Italians and Greeks and Lebanese anymore. They were Aussies quicker than you could have believed. The fact that none of us belong here – except the Originals – and all of us drifted in from somewhere else makes Australia such an interesting melting pot. And a good melting pot.

I worked on the railways at one stage, laying down a new line between Lidcombe and Granville. I was working with my

The fact that none of us belong here – except the Originals – makes Australia such an interesting melting pot ...

Greek milk bars revolutionised what we ate and how we socialised in Australia. In the 1950s they brought us the hamburger, the milkshake and the juke box. This is the Niagara Café in Gundagai, NSW.

mate Phil. It was us two, plus twenty-eight New Australians. They were mainly Italians and a few Yugoslavs, and many spoke almost no English.

That was an incredibly hot job, and there wasn't much in the way of OHS back then. The trains would still be running while we worked, though they'd slow down when they saw us on the tracks, and we'd step back a bit.

Me and Phil became honorary Italians, learnt a bit of the language, and admired their food. We'd always bring a sandwich in a brown paper bag, but they'd have elaborate lunchboxes filled with cooked food and all sorts of interesting stuff. Wasn't hard to see they were taking mealtimes a fair bit more seriously than us.

A couple of them would eat with their left arm held up, wrapped around their lunch to hide it. And Phil and I would wonder what part of the world they came from, where you had to protect your food or someone was going to take it. Still, pretty well all the guys on that crew laughed a lot, and we had plenty of fun.

My favourite bloke was a tiny little Italian named Gino. He was a pocket Hercules and when the trains slowed down and crept past, he always stood on a pile of gravel or a couple of railway sleepers to get to the same height as the rest of us, and he'd whip off his shirt, puff out his chest and sing out at the girls: 'Hello baby! Hello baby!'

One time a train came almost to a complete stop and I heard him yell, 'Hello, baby. Meet me tonight. I gift to you one jiggi-jiggi.' Gino didn't get a reply, and I'm sure the object of his affections was real pleased when the train started up again. But we couldn't help but laugh at our pocket Hercules.

Usi, Usi, Usi – Oi! Oi! Oi!

I can never remember as a teenager, or any time later, hearing anyone criticise any sportsman or sportswoman because their name sounded Polish or Russian or Italian. If a guy was the five-eighth for the Australian rugby league team, it didn't matter where he came from. George Peponis was born in Greece and became the captain of the Australian rugby league team, the Kangaroos. He was a doctor too. Talk about an overachiever. Because of people like him and Aussie rules legend Robert 'Dipper' DiPierdomenico, and hundreds more, European names started to become familiar and accepted, and soon names like Smith, Hogan, Peponis and DiPierdomenico were also being joined by names from every other part of the world.

We've largely avoided ghettos in Australia. People from almost every country all walk around and mingle. Young kids, wherever they come from, soon sound exactly like everyone else here. They develop what I call an Australian attitude: laid-back, easy-going, with a tendency to laugh a lot and not take anything too seriously.

We had no chance of being anything other than laid-back really. The Original Australians are laid-back, hilariously funny people, and the Poms have a brilliant understanding of comedy and, as their Empire and influence have faded, they've learnt to become at least a little laid-back themselves.

But such things take time. When the boat people started coming here after the Vietnam War – which we went to, war being our favourite pastime – many Australians resented them. I have a T-shirt with a cartoon of an Indigenous person saying, 'So you're complaining about the boat people. Not so funny now, is it?'

It took a while, but we realised how wrong we were about the Vietnamese. You go to other countries like Spain, Italy and Japan, and most of the people there were born there. But in Australia, you can look around and it's sort of like we're all refos. I think it's great.

We had no chance of being anything other than laid-back, really. The Original Australians are laid-back, hilariously funny people ...

Peter Bol stopped the nation when he made the 800-metre final in the Tokyo Olympics. He went on to take silver at the 2022 Commonwealth Games.

Each generation opens up a little more, and opens us up a little more too. There is always the shock of the new, and that's what African arrivals are facing to some extent now, but it will improve quickly.

In 2021, we tuned in by the millions to watch Peter Bol, the Sudanese-born Australian sprinter who made the final of the 800 metres at the Tokyo Olympic Games. He gave a terrific speech afterwards in the broadest Aussie accent, and we were proud as Punch. Less than a year later he brought home silver from the Commonwealth Games in Birmingham.

Pakistani-born cricketer Usman Khawaja returned to the Australian batting line-up after a couple of years for the fourth test in the 2021–22 Ashes series. Before he'd even hit a single ball, the crowd gave him a standing ovation. And he paid them back by hitting a couple of centuries. We'd love anyone who did that for Australia, but to hear thousands replacing our famous chant of 'Aussie, Aussie, Aussie – Oi! Oi! Oi!' with 'Usi, Usi, Usi – Oi! Oi! Oi!' was magic. We've come a bloody long way.

It's not perfect, but immigration has worked better here than almost anywhere else. No matter what colour or creed, no matter where they are from, people very rapidly become Australians. Some of the most Australian people I know are of Greek or Italian origin. They are loyal supporters of their footy club, and stick by each other. They like to gamble, they like to drink, and they sing and dance. The Poms weren't nearly as much into that sort of thing.

It's happened in my lifetime. I've seen that radical change from radical racism to radical acceptance. Look at the speed of it. Other places took hundreds of years to improve the situation – or not. We went from a prison farm to a very progressive, very diverse nation in virtually two lifetimes. Now we have 27 million or so people living in pretty good harmony. We didn't get to that number by super-breeding. We did it by bringing them in from all over the world. What a triumph!

'Usi, Usi, Usi – Oi! Oi! Oi!'

CHAPTER 2

War and (a Little Bit of) Peace

You name it, we turned up

Australia's only claim to fame in the early days was that, since we'd been a prison colony, we were a pretty hardy bunch. So we became famous for providing soldiers. Anywhere you had a war, Australians would turn up. Every Aussie bloke wanted to go, didn't seem to matter how young, or how old. It was a chance to travel, get fed, get paid and see some action. We loved our wars: the Crimean, the American Civil War, the Boer War, World Wars I and II, Korea, Vietnam, Iraq, Afghanistan. You name it, we turned up. That was our thing. Though we did squeeze in a bit of action on the home front too …

Mutinous from the start

In 1789, in the southern Pacific Ocean, English mariner and lieutenant Fletcher Christian, sailing on Her Majesty's Ship the *Bounty*, famously led a mutiny against Captain William Bligh. Set adrift in a small open boat, Bligh and eighteen loyal crewmen managed to navigate for 6500 kilometres to Australia and then what is now Indonesia. There weren't any Australians involved, but Bligh had a reputation for cruelty and was working for the British crown. And it was the British crown that had sent its convicts to the ends of the earth. So facing up to Bligh was appealing to Australians.

Challenging authority is in our nature, so we backed Christian and his mob. And later when Bligh became

---

How to Speak 'STRAYAN

blue

A fight. *Putting on a blue*, or thumping people, was the answer to everything back in the day. Not so much now. Maybe it's because we're better at conversation, and just better people generally. Or maybe it's because we're copying the Americans and suing people instead. Contingency lawyers! We never had those in Australia. Lawyers couldn't advertise either. Now they are everywhere, on billboards and on the radio. It's even worse in America. You see ads saying: 'If you've had an accident, if you've been in an accident, if you've seen an accident, if you've even heard about an accident, we can get you money.' They're relentless, on everything, day after day.

A rare original photo taken on the Bounty just before the mutiny. Well sort of – it's from the 1935 film starring Charles Laughton and Clark Gable. Charles Laughton – sorry, Captain Bligh – ended up running Australia for a while.

Governor of New South Wales, we took a tip from Christian and overthrew Bligh again, in the so-called Rum Rebellion of 1808. At the time rum was the New South Wales currency. You could drink your pay directly and cut out the middle man. So Australian. When Bligh tried to halt this practice, the military garrison, the New South Wales Corp, which controlled the rum trade, overthrew him. Alas, Governor Lachlan Macquarie arrived in 1810, took control back from the 'Rum Corps', and decided alcohol wasn't the best medium of exchange. He went for coins instead.

The Rum Rebellion was our only military coup d'état, though we also gave the idea a bit of a burl forty-six years later at the Eureka Stockade, near Ballarat in Victoria. There, gold miners fought with the colonial forces over the high cost

This was possibly Australia's first political cartoon, even if there aren't many laughs in it. It depicts Governor William Bligh as a coward, hiding under the bed when the Rum Corps came for him, in what was our first and only coup d'etat.

of mining licences and various other gripes. About twenty-seven people died, most of them rebels, but their leader, Peter Lalor, eventually became Speaker of the Victorian Legislative Assembly. It always was a land of opportunity!

Our first real wars

We fought in the Crimean War from 1853, even though we were still considered a convict colony. Some guys went off to the American Civil War not too long after. A Confederacy ship called *Shenandoah* landed in Melbourne, and the guys on it looked around at all these no-hopers and said, 'Would you like to travel?'

'Oh yeah!'

'And would you like to shoot at people too?'

'Yeah, even better.'

LEADING
THE WAY

In 1894 South Australia became the first Australian colony, and the second place in the world, behind New Zealand, where women won the right to vote. And when we federated in 1901, women gained the vote nationally. So, in world terms, Australian women were ahead of women in most other countries. In fact, it was women who kept the place running for many decades because all our boofheads were always rushing off to a war somewhere.

Australian performer Helen Reddy co-wrote and sang the English-speaking world's feminist anthem, 'I Am Woman'. Australia introduced equal pay in the early 1970s, though in practice we've still got a way to go. We've made progress in quite a few other areas too. To be honest, our country's still a bit on the chauvinist side, but we're working on it.

Helen Reddy (foreground) and those ever-cheerful ladies from the Women's Suffrage League of SA. Their ideas were not a million miles apart, but Helen was much more entertaining.

How to Speak 'STRAYAN

digger

Our soldiers were *diggers*. It was possibly because they dug trenches in World War I, though everyone else dug trenches too. Calling someone 'digger' is still a sign of respect.

I think they got more than forty recruits right out of Melbourne. Over a hundred Aussies overall fought in the the Civil War. Some of them, when they got into American waters to join the Confederate side, were stuck in a naval blockade. 'Well, we didn't come all this way to sit on deck and sun ourselves,' they said, so they jumped ship and joined the Union Army. They didn't care what side they were on; they just wanted a blue. But it was probably handy for those ship-jumpers that they were able to justify themselves a bit when they learnt about slavery and discovered they were on the side that was against it.

The Boer War, which kicked off in 1899 with the British Empire taking on a couple of Dutch-dominated South African republics, was just another of the many stoushes we rushed off to. Each Australian state sent its own troops, but it was Queenslanders who found out first there was a war going on. 'We'll be in that!' they said. An uncle of my mum, Uncle Dick, went off to South Africa for that one.

We were getting the reputation that, if you were looking for mercenaries, there was this joint down south that'd had all these crims and hard types, and they loved wars. And that became a badge of pride, that we produced good mercenaries.

Why were they so good? I think it was because they lived the rural life and could ride horses and shoot. That was pretty well the job description back then: 'Must be able to ride a horse and shoot. Preference given to candidates prepared to travel to far-off, exotic lands, and meet far-off, exotic people, and kill them.'

Sticking it out in the not-so-great war

We solidified our war reputation in World War I, joining our New Zealand brothers in that stoush, and together putting in a bloody good performance.

I learnt a lot about it when we filmed *Anzacs*, the 1985 television series. I played recruit Pat Cleary, who was fighting in Gallipoli and then in the Somme campaign around Pozières in France. I was told that at one stage in the Battle of the Somme the Anzacs made up 70 percent of the front line, despite having only 25 percent of the troops there.

On the set of Anzacs with Andrew Clarke – a wonderful and educational experience.

WE LOVE OUR VEGEMITE

He's doing his bit for his Dad...

The richest food source
of the combined
Vitamins B¹ B² and P.P.

(the anti-pellagric factor)

Young Peter loves Vegemite . . . and his mother loves giving it to him . . . but he's not getting so much these days, as his mother says: "It's nearly all going to Daddy, Peter." And she's right! The Vegemite is needed for our fighting men.

As you know, Vegemite is a concentrated extract of yeast, which contains three vital vitamins—B¹, B² and P.P. (the anti-pellagric factor). That is why Vegemite is so necessary to our fighting men at home and overseas.

B¹ — is the Nerve Vitamin. To have a strong, well stomach, and a normal, healthy intestinal tract, we need an ample supply of vitamin B¹. Vegemite is one of the richest natural food sources of this vitamin.

B² — is the Growth Vitamin. When you get too little of the vitamin B² it means poor growth and under-

nourishment. Vegemite is rich in this vitamin B². It helps proper growth and all-round development of the body.

P.P.— (anti-pellagric factor). Vegemite keeps skin clear and healthy because it supplies the system with the right amount of the skin-clearing vitamin known as P.P. Yes! Vegemite is a concentrated food. Rich food and energy values are packed into Vegemite.

So if you notice less Vegemite in your local shop, just remember that until we have won this war a lot of it will be going to the troops! Vegemite—the concentrated extract of yeast — the richest food source of the combined vitamins B¹, B² and P.P. (anti-pellagric factor). The food that helps keep the troops fighting.

VEGEMITE *is with the Troops!*

The 1920s were called the Roaring Twenties overseas. I'm not sure how much they roared here. Women outnumbered blokes by a huge margin because our menfolk had taken such a hit in the war. Still, we didn't waste our time: we invented Vegemite, an almost black spread concocted from brewer's yeast and a range of vegetable and spice extracts.

This magical goop was first produced in 1923, and it remains one of the great Australian products. I have it every morning for breakfast, even when I'm in LA. Why? Because basically it's salt, and who doesn't like salt? And also because a famous advertising jingle drummed it into us from the very start:

> We're happy little Vegemites, as bright as bright can be,
> We all enjoy our Vegemite for breakfast, lunch and tea,
> Our mummy says we're growing stronger every single week,
> Because we love our Vegemite, we all adore our Vegemite —
> It puts a rose in every cheek!
> We're growing stronger every week!

I can still sing it because it was on the radio all the time, and in very early ads on television. To be a 'Happy Little Vegemite' came to mean you were content.

In other parts of the Western world, Vegemite is known as a very Australian, very perplexing, thing. People there think it's terrible because they put it on too thick. I've even seen American friends grab a spoon and lob a mouthful in before I've had time to stop them. Their reaction is always entertaining.

My son Chance has been trying to teach his LA mates how to use it properly. He loves the stuff. In fact, he got angry recently because there was Marmite in the house. Me handing confidential government files to the Russians would be less treasonous in his eyes than giving shelf space to Marmite. Vegemite'll do that to you.

furphy

A term for a story that turns out to be false. During World War I information was locked down tight, but rumours would travel with the Furphy-brand carts that brought the troops water. The term is still used in the newspaper trade, when they chase up a story and find out there's nothing in it.

We got slaughtered wholesale, of course, just as we did at Gallipoli, thanks to having British officers. It was then we realised we needed our own people in charge, not these idiots, because it was the British that landed us at Gallipoli, at the bottom of a cliff in the worst possible spot. Why were we even over there fighting the Turks? Our guys didn't really know who the Turks were. We heard 'Turkey' and thought of the bird. But suddenly we were at war and losing thousands of lives.

Gallipoli is the one we still most talk about. Like the infamous expedition led by Robert O'Hara Burke and William John Wills, which set out in 1860 to cross Australia from south to north and ended with almost everyone perishing in the outback, Gallipoli is one of those losing missions that somehow, with our national psyche, we celebrate more than we celebrate our victories. With Gallipoli, it was because of the way those Anzacs stuck it out, which we still refer to as the *Anzac spirit*. They were dumped in an unwinnable situation. And they hung in there and tried to do the impossible. It's the underdog thing. You know, 'Stupid Pommies put us here, so we're going to have to get out of it on our own.'

Australians wouldn't be nearly as quick to sign up for an overseas war nowadays, at least not one fighting an enemy we don't really know for a cause that isn't crystal clear. Not at all. Back then, the main attraction was travelling. Now it's easier to just jump on a cheap flight.

Round 2: War comes closer to home

Nineteen-thirty-nine: the year World War II began and the year I was born.

The war started coming close to home from early 1942, when the Japanese took Singapore, capturing a large number of Australian troops. They bombed Darwin a few days later and soon after sent midget submarines into Sydney Harbour. That really told us how close the threat was coming. By then we had our bomb shelter and darkened blinds. The Japanese were set on invading our country because we'd rushed off to help Britain, and most of our troops were up in Europe and Africa, busy fighting the Germans and Italians. And doing well, thanks very much.

THE COATHANGER

Another great thing we squeezed in between the world wars was the Sydney Harbour Bridge. It opened in 1932. I'd eventually work on it, but long before that I'd regularly travel over it and be amazed by its size and the complexity of its construction. Usually, I'd be on my way to the beach. From Granville, in the Western Suburbs, where I lived, we'd take a train into the city and across the Bridge, then we'd get a tram down to Balmoral Beach. That was a favourite family trip. Balmoral wasn't a surf beach, but we'd regularly make our way there. There was a tram to Bondi Beach too, but for some reason from Granville it worked out easier to go to Balmoral.

The Harbour Bridge has been replaced by the Opera House as the major city icon, at least in the sense that anytime you see an overseas news report about Sydney it's there in the background. But how lucky are we to have two symbols that allow anyone in the world to identify our city. And I worked on one of them and watched the other one grow.

There's no better view in the world than from the top of the Harbour Bridge, and working there spoilt me. You were out in the sun, getting paid, with blokes who were great mates. I was very content there.

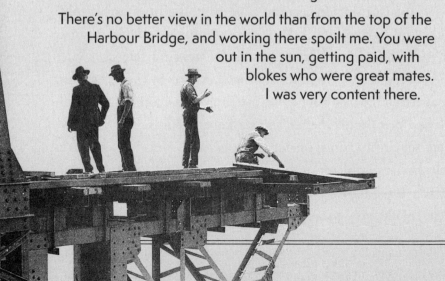

Field Marshal Erwin Rommel often praised the Anzac troops and even supposedly said: 'If I had to invade Hell, I'd use Australian troops. And if I had to hold it, I'd use New Zealanders.' The Australians admired Rommel. He wasn't a Nazi, he was a professional soldier, and a very good one, making his mark as a leader years before anyone had even heard of the tyrant with the silly moustache. He may even have been involved in a 1944 plot to kill Hitler, which, alas, failed.

Anyway, we might have been fighting the Germans and Italians, but we were much more prejudiced against Japan. Sure, they were the ones bombing us, but it was also because they looked different. They were called 'the yellow peril' in all our propaganda. It was easy for people to believe the horde was on its way down here and would treat us with the cruelty they had shown to other people they had conquered.

The Yanks, who didn't think much of the Japanese either, largely on account of Pearl Harbor, cut them off in the Battle of the Coral Sea (with some help from the Royal Australian Navy and Air Force) and sank enough of their ships to turn the tide. By the end of 1942, Australian troops were pushing the Japanese back in New Guinea and the threat of invasion had passed.

Australia takes on America

During World War II, Australians generally loved the Americans. After all, they saved our bacon. If you were an American soldier stationed in Australia in the 1940s, you couldn't buy a meal or a drink, because every regular punter wanted to shout you. It didn't matter if you were white, black or purple.

A bit of official crawling ... still, the Yanks were super popular, most of the time, when they turned up here during World War II.

Our troops were often a lot less happy about that, because Aussie women were taking a shine to the Yanks, who had more money, better-looking uniforms and spoke with that accent we'd all heard in the movies.

This led to the Battle of Brisbane, when Aussie troops and some civilian supporters took on the US military in a series of street fights over two nights in 1942. Hundreds were injured and at least one person died, and authorities censored it all because it didn't look good to be fighting your allies rather than your enemy.

Incidents like this – and it wasn't the only one – didn't stop a lot of Australian women carousing with US troops. Many got pregnant and/or married their Yank soldier and headed off to the States at war's end. The weird thing was that a lot of these war brides left our shores thinking that, because their husband was handsome and had an American accent, they were off to a mansion in Beverly Hills or a New York penthouse. And they ended up in rural Oklahoma, or some other dirt-poor, dusty, windswept joint.

Australia takes on Japan and Italy

My father was stationed at Cowra, New South Wales, in 1944, when Japanese prisoners of war organised a mass breakout. There were 1104 POWs involved in a banzai charge. Many were killed, but hundreds escaped into the bush. Dad was a staff sergeant during the war, the guy you went to to get all your equipment. But obviously the Australian Army didn't have a lot of equipment at the time, because the prison guards found that guns were in especially short supply. When Dad

A rare shot of my dad smiling. He probably wasn't aware when the picture was taken that he was expected to fight the Japanese with a 9-iron.

was roped in, like everyone else, to help look for the escapees, his superiors handed out golf clubs instead. So there was Dad, and a mate, the two of them going through the bush looking for Japanese POWs with a sand wedge and a putting iron.

It was quite a different story with our Italian POWs. In a camp outside Myrtleford in Victoria, there was supposedly one guard for every forty Italian soldiers, because the Italian soldiers showed no interest in escaping. Most of them preferred to be in a prisoner-of-war camp in Australia, where the weather was good and there was decent food, than back home where conditions were awful and they'd have to rejoin a war they didn't believe in.

The guards knew it too, and one night one of them took a whole lot of prisoners with him in a truck to the Myrtleford pub, where they all got drunk. None of the prisoners was quite

DON'T BLAME
CHARLIE

We hated the Japanese well into the 1960s. It's hard to imagine because we get on so well today. Racism is stupid. None of the people who bombed Australia, and none of the people whose idea it was to bomb it, are still alive. (If they were in a plane, they had to be twenty years old back then, and if they were making the decisions, they had to be older again; that would make them well over a hundred now.) I may as well blame Charlie, who runs my local Japanese restaurant (and looks after me very well). He's about forty.

My grand-dog – the big, boofy bitzer owned by my daughter Loren and her four sons – is named after the anime character Haku. Anime was probably the best thing that happened for relations with the Japanese, as the younger ones now are all into it. Chance, my youngest, couldn't wait to visit Japan, to get into the world of ninjas, anime, Japanese punk bands and all that. He loves Japan. It's a very cool place.

Anyone who still resents Japanese people because of the sins of their forefathers should never forget the many sins of ours, starting with how they treated our First Nations people. Racism is based on clinging on to ancestry, instead of dealing with people as you find them. Good riddance to that.

as drunk as the guard, however, so the Italians loaded him into the truck and drove it back, then put him to bed in his hut before returning to their dorms. I think they were what we'd call 'model prisoners'.

The future starts here

I remember the victory celebrations in 1945. I'd lived my entire life in wartime until then. Everyone was out on the street cheering. There were tanks going along Parramatta Road, which was only a block away, together with marching bands and soldiers in uniform.

We took all the black blinds off the windows and filled in the trench that was our bomb shelter. I was only five at that time, but I knew something big was happening, and the future was looking good.

CHAPTER 3

A Sporting Chance

First objective: beat the Poms

In the early days, Australians had no real identity, except as soldiers. We were very proud of our young men who had died, of our Anzac spirit, and of our often match-winning performances on the battlefield. But we had nothing else to set us apart – except sport.

While we'd been to more wars than almost any other country on the planet, we couldn't fight Britain. That just wouldn't have been on. So, we had to beat England at cricket, which we managed to do as early as 1882. There's a great pleasure in caning a country at a sport they invented, and particularly when it's England. It's a revenge thing, whether we acknowledge it or not, a product of the cultural-cringe inferiority complex that we had bred into us from the start.

ABOVE: The Australian cricket team of 1882, off to England to beat the beloved enemy in what would later be known as the first Ashes test match.

LEFT: The Ashes urn, which was presented to England's captain, Ivo Bligh, by a group of Melbourne women, after our tourists clobbered the Pommies on their own turf.

Sport always comes first – and last

In late April 2022, I was sitting in a garden in northern Sydney, reading the newspaper (like older people still do). Splashed right across the front page was a photo of some guys in footy jumpers, and the back thirteen pages were all sport. In the middle was a ten-page racing form guide. So there were twenty-four pages dedicated to sport in that one weekday edition. The *LA Times* has about three pages, in total, to cover baseball, basketball, American football and everything else.

That comparison sums up just how important sport is in Australia. It's an absolutely integral part of our psyche. Even our newspapers' crossword clues have more sport in them than anyone else's. It seems like the Yanks' Super Bowl doesn't get as much press as our lady lawn bowlers – though I'll admit their half-time entertainment is slightly more impressive.

> *It seems like the Yanks' Super Bowl doesn't get as much press as our lady lawn bowlers.*

I think our sporting prowess is only matched, on a pro rata basis, by New Zealand, an even smaller country that has had world champions in all sorts of team and individual sports. So where did our will to win come from? From us feeling like we were on the back foot from the start. The battlefield was the first place where we could prove ourselves, and the sporting field became the second.

Not that we haven't had some pretty good thinkers in this country too. Some pretty handy inventions have come out of here: the boomerang, the woomera, the stump-jump plough, the rotary hoist, Cochlear implants, Wi-Fi and lots more. But we weren't necessarily as proud of our thinkers, or our inventors, or our artists, as we were of our sportsmen and women. When politician John Brown greenlit my 'shrimp on the barbie' television advertisements in 1986 to attract visitors to Australia, he was the federal Minister for Sport and Tourism. Tourism might have been the biggest industry in the world, but sport came first. And many Australians would say, 'Yeah, fair enough.'

The stump-jump plough, part of a great tradition from the boomerang to the Hills rotary hoist and Wi-Fi.

Dreaming of greatness
on the footy field

Every Australian, just about, has played grassroots sport and dreamt of greatness, imagining they were in a giant stadium in front of adoring crowds, not in a windy park in front of a few family and friends who've turned up more to give the dog an outing than to watch the game. I'm no exception.

When I worked on the Harbour Bridge in the 1960s, we had a rugby league team and used to compete in the Sydney Business Houses competition. Biggish companies and organisations would put together footy teams and we'd play on Sundays. Everyone in our team worked up there on the Bridge except for a few ring-in wharfies from the Harbour View Hotel, where we all went drinking on a Friday night. The competition ran from the 1950s until the 1970s, and there were countless similar ones in all sorts of sports. I suspect the reason companies don't organise nearly as many weekend

fit as a mallee bull

I never knew what a mallee bull was, but this phrase is still used, particularly for athletes. A footballer who is big, strong and still going hard towards the end of the match, is *as fit as a mallee bull*. And you don't want to stand in the way.

teams and competitions these days is because they're too worried about liability. Shame.

Anyway, I played in this comp right through my twenties, stopping soon after I began appearing on television as the comic relief on the TV show *A Current Affair*. Back in my day, a rugby league team was dominated by the forwards, who were big bulky blokes whose job it was to push hard in the scrums and, in general play, run the ball, kamikaze-style, right down the middle. They had to do this with no thought of personal safety, in order to soften up the other side. And they took the brunt of the punishment when the other side was doing the same. The team also had backs, who tended in those days to be lighter and quicker. Nowadays everyone's enormous, but back then there was a position for smaller, wiry guys like me. If I could stay out of trouble, I could contribute quite a bit by just being quick.

Our coach said to me, 'You're an athlete in a footy jumper.'

What he meant by that was, *You're quick on your feet, which is just as well, because you don't have much in the way of other skills.* Still, quick was good and I scored quite a few tries for our team, and we managed to win the premiership in our first season.

A physical challenge

That competition was usually great fun, though there were a couple of teams we never enjoyed playing. One was Austral Bronze. That was a big foundry, and their team was tough, and didn't mind putting on the biff. But it was the Sydney Deaf Rugby League Football Club, which came into the comp in 1966, that would make the boys whisper, 'Oh shit, guess who we're playing tomorrow.'

Sydney Deaf were the toughest, sneakiest team around. Every time you were tackled and then stood up to play the ball, you just knew you were going to get hit again with a late shot. They did it every time and would just shrug their shoulders as if to say, 'I never heard the whistle.' Of course, they didn't hear the whistle, they were deaf. But, hey, they knew exactly what was going on. And just because you're deaf, doesn't mean you can't be six foot two and built like a brick shithouse.

This team really had something to prove. It was like they were saying, *Yeah, okay, we might be deaf, but we're not bad at this.* I knew a couple of them who were very short of hearing but could lipread and talk a bit. They thought it was hilarious, what they could get away with. As a team they weren't very well coordinated because communication was a problem. But their combination of skill, toughness and terror meant they'd often run second or third in the premiership. And God, they brought on the bruises.

RING-INS AND STIFF ARMS

The Sydney Business Houses eligibility rules weren't that strict and, although Bridge workers were always the backbone of our rugby league team, we'd usually front up with a few wharfies, or even a cop or two, because we were always short of people. And I'd bring the guy next door because another thing we were always short of was talent. We didn't have a good kicker and this bloke, Roy Mayberry, could slot it between the posts from anywhere on the field.

Roy worked at Australian Aluminium, and one time when I owed him a favour or two I agreed to make up the numbers in one of their lunchtime social matches. His team of blue-collar workers were playing the Australian Aluminium office, which sounded like a pretty easy day out. We assumed we'd be up against a bunch of pasty, white-collared clerks and went in pretty cocky, and I was expecting to score a few meat pies (tries).

Then the other side walked onto the field. At that point I realised the Australian Aluminium office had a couple of ring-ins too and they were not pasty, white-collared clerks. They were the McMartins, huge twin brothers who were stars in first grade (John with the Parramatta Eels and Mal with the Penrith Panthers).

This didn't seem fair at all. These ring-ins weren't somebody's next-door neighbour, or a mate from the pub, or the younger brother of the guy from the purchasing office down the hall. They were real ring-ins. The office was going to stick it to the workers, when it was supposed to be the other way around.

The game was a blur. All I remembered afterwards was getting the ball and taking off with John McMartin, the hooker, chasing me and Mal McMartin, the centre, still in front of me. I don't know if they did it deliberately, but they managed to hit me at exactly the same time from opposite directions, turning me into a McMartin sandwich. I did get up, eventually, but I didn't know what planet I was on.

It was another reminder that there was a big difference between what I was playing and what the pros were playing. I don't remember the score, but we were trounced. Thrashed. Whooped. Walloped.

Attracting attention

I was still playing for the Harbour Bridge team after I'd turned thirty, but there were two problems with this.

The first was that by then my kids were also playing rugby league and I'd coach them in the backyard. They'd play on Saturdays and come to watch me on Sundays, and it became pretty obvious that they were getting better and I'd already peaked. How was I going to get them to listen to my advice if they realised that was the case?

The other problem in the twilight of my football career was that I'd started appearing on television. Although our competition was a long way short of first grade, there were still some pretty big, and pretty angry, players pulling on a jersey. And nothing seemed to motivate a pretty big, and pretty angry, player as much as knowing the guy opposite him was on the telly.

I started getting a lot more attention, and not in a good way. It happened every game. People'd put two and two together, even dumb forwards: *It's the Harbour Bridge footy team, and that guy looks just like the guy on the telly who all the papers say works on the Bridge. So it must be the same bloke and, therefore, I should flatten him.*

Every time I got the ball, some huge front-rower would go straight for me and clobber me or, if they had the ball, would swerve well out of their way so they could run right over the top of me.

I guess it was very hard for me to be doing something more Australian than playing rugby league for the Sydney Harbour

tall poppy

If you get a little bit too far ahead, then you're a *tall poppy*. Our egalitarian nature is great, and plays out in various ways. For example, we're always quick to remind people that they're not more important than anyone else, no matter what their job is, or who their parents are, or where they went to school. The downside of this is the *tall-poppy syndrome*: We're all equal and we're all together, but don't you dare succeed too much. Yeah, I've occasionally copped some of that myself, but on balance I've been treated pretty bloody well.

Bridge football team. And I guess it was very hard for them to be more Australian than to boast at their building site on Monday morning about mowing down a tall poppy. *Hey, you know that guy who does the funny bits at the end of* A Current Affair? *I knocked his lights out yesterday!*

I knew it was time to give it all away. But it's worth mentioning that, even after a particularly violent game, once the full-time whistle sounded, everyone was best of mates. You could go to the pub with a bunch of blokes who had just shoulder-charged your neck, rubbed your face into the mud with the underside of their boots, and stiff-armed you across the eye sockets, and laugh about it all while sinking a few schooners.

Once the whistle sounded, what had happened on the field stayed there.

The wild Whirler

To be fair though, we had a couple of hard men in our team too. One of them we called The Whirler. That was because when he worked on the Bridge he wore overalls with 'Whirler' written on the chest pocket. He'd got those overalls years earlier when he'd had a job at a carnival – The Whirler was some kind of crazy ride – and he was determined to wear them to work until they were worn away to nothing. The Whirler was my rugby league partner in the 'centres'. He was a wild man, which is why I'll just use his nickname.

We were playing the semi-final. It wasn't first grade, and we weren't playing for sheep stations, but it was important for us to win, and that meant maintaining a bit of discipline so we could have all thirteen players on the field throughout the game. But The Whirler didn't really think that way.

So, we're still in the opening minute, and he tackles one bloke right round the head and very nearly removes it. And then, about three minutes later, he buries another one face first into the turf. It's an illegal spear tackle, legs in the air, the full catastrophe. Surprise, surprise, the ref sends him off.

Next thing you know he's walking up to our club president on the sideline. Now, our club president we called Roughy, because he had a rough head. He was the Bridge carpenter who'd eventually make my fake knives and other props in his workshop for my *New Faces* appearance. Anyway, The Whirler stares at him with the angriest face and seethes, 'A man can only take so much.'

Roughy looks at him in astonishment and replies, 'Mate, you were on the field for about four minutes and you nearly killed two people.'

The Whirler keeps shaking his head and swearing. The thing is he sees himself as the victim in all this, rather than the two innocent people he's clobbered. *A man can only take so much!*

He was a great character, The Whirler. He was the type who'd work hard and quietly all week without complaint and then all his frustrations with the boss, his arguments with the missus, and problems with the kids and the landlord would come out on the footy field. Sunday's game would be this huge, violent release of tension. You did well to spot blokes like that on the other side and stay out of their way. As I've said elsewhere, Australians were originally all about war, and mostly replaced that with sport. But sometimes the two were very similar.

Aussie rules, ok?

I was amazed to learn that Australian Rules Football was codified as long ago as 1859. It was partly based on Gaelic football, sure. But there's a theory that First Nations people in the southern part of what became Victoria had a game called Marn Grook that also influenced Aussie Rules. Whatever the true story, our First Nations people have always been very good at it.

It's no surprise that someone came up with a game that took advantage of our wide-open spaces. We have so much room, more than just about anyone else, and AFL has the biggest field of any team ball sport. The grounds can be 185 metres, end to end, and 155 metres side to side. That's almost twice the length of a rugby league field, and more than twice the width.

Aussie Rules is one of the few mainstream sports I haven't played. Nobody was into it in New South Wales or in Queensland when I was a kid, so nobody gave it the respect it deserved. Including me, until much later, when I started doing my television show out of Melbourne. At first I thought I might be able to avoid the topic … but what was I thinking? In Melbourne their second question is always, 'What team do you support?' It would be their first question, but they are usually polite enough to start by asking your name.

If you don't support a team they think there's something wrong with you, so I knew I had to get one, real quick. I asked one of the Channel 9 commentators, Kevin Sheedy. He recommended the Richmond Tigers. He'd been a champion player for the team himself, so probably wasn't going to give me any other suggestion. I got myself down to a game so I knew what was going on, and the Tigers became my team. Watching it up close, I realised it was a very different game from the one I'd seen on TV, because there's so much strategy across the whole field. I started watching a lot of it and became a genuine fan.

I love that the game is played over such a huge area and is so fast. There are no scrums or silly stoppages. It's nonstop and the guys are so fit and athletic and skilful. You can make it big in rugby league if you've got a concrete head and you like ploughing into people. But in Aussie Rules, no, you need a range of talents.

It's little wonder the sport finally sneaked into Sydney in the early 1980s with the transformation of South Melbourne into the Sydney Swans. I even watch a bit of coverage of AFL in America. They always say 'These Aussies don't wear helmets or padded uniforms, they get around in shorts and singlets. They're tougher than us. And such little shorts!'

The only thing I don't like about AFL is that the Poms don't play it. That means we can't beat them at it.

PLAIN
SAILING

I once read that as early as the 1820s the working boats in Sydney Harbour used to race each other. And if that's true, you can be pretty sure that those on board, and those on the shore, were having a punt on the results.

A few years later Launceston, Tasmania, gave the country its first proper yacht club, the Tamar Yacht Club. That was in 1837, and we remain pretty boat crazy. It makes sense given we have so much shoreline, and beautiful harbours. The annual Sydney Hobart Yacht Race is one of the great races, but nothing has ever stopped the country quite like when we took the America's Cup off the Yanks in 1983. No one had ever done it in 132 years of trying, mainly because the rules were set up to make sure the Americans always won.

The final, deciding race was in the early hours of the morning and we all stayed up to watch *Australia II* take on the American boat *Liberty*. When *Australia II* won, thanks partly to its famous winged keel, we all knew it was a great achievement for our little pissant island. Our then prime minister, Bob Hawke, famously said he couldn't make it a public holiday, because that was a state matter, but added, 'Any boss who sacks anyone for not turning up today is a bum.' What a day! I remember it as clearly as if it just happened.

Big Bash

This of course is the name of our national Twenty20 cricket competition. I just love the directness of calling something the *Big Bash*. They don't fool around, it's the Big Bash. Straight to the point. That's very Australian. Occasionally when I watch, I see the camera closing in on the bowler's face. They're just shaking their heads, going, 'Yeah. What can we do?' Well, it's the Big Bash, mate, not the Big Bowl. You're there to take your punishment, you're there to put balls up for guys to hit out of the ground. We don't care about you!

Shoulda coulda won the bloody thing

We were always sports mad, but I consider the 1956 Olympics in Melbourne to be the event that pushed things up a notch. It truly turned us into a sporting nation. More than that, it made us sports maniacs.

Melbourne was the perfect place to have our first Olympics. If you put on a game of checkers in Melbourne, you'll get a crowd. Melburnians are the most going-out people on the planet, and the most supportive sports fans around.

I remember the first week of the 1956 Olympics with extraordinary pride. There was a battle in the medal count between three nations: the Soviet Union, the USA and Australia. And naturally we expected Australia to stay in front, despite the fact that Russia had 220 million people, America had 170 million and we had less than 10 million. We were up there with them because we loved our sport more than they did.

We were strongest in the swimming, of course. We never normally made much of a dint in the athletics, but in the 1950s we had the Golden Girls, including Marjorie Jackson, known as the Lithgow Flash, who won gold in the 100 metres and 200 metres sprints at Helsinki in 1952, and Betty Cuthbert, who won gold medals in the same events in 1956. She teamed up with Fleur Mellor, Norma Croker and Shirley Strickland to grab another gold in the 4 x 100 metres relay.

There was always someone else's TV to watch if you didn't have your own.

Australia got television in time for the Olympics. The Hogan family didn't have a set, but we used to go each day and stand in the street outside Clay's Radio Store to watch. And there'd always be a crowd looking through that shop window, staring at this one little black-and-white television set. Clay's would broadcast the sound outside through a small speaker, and we'd cheer our heads off when Australians came through.

In the end, Australia finished third behind the USSR and the US, and won more than twice as many golds as Great Britain.

Party of the millennium

At the Summer Olympics in Sydney in 2000, we proved yet again that we could run huge sporting events better than just about anyone, and we could also give the world the most beautiful harbour city as a backdrop, as well as its most enthusiastic spectators.

My old mate and TV producer Peter Faiman – who did *The Paul Hogan Show* and *Crocodile Dundee* – directed the opening and closing television broadcasts, which is why it all looked so wonderful. I ended up in the closing ceremony, which was certainly the best way to see it. Not sure though why I was placed next to Greg Norman as we sang the national anthem. We were trying to attract tourism from across the world and we had two Australians side by side, one associated with crocodiles and the other nicknamed the Great White Shark.

Sydney 2000 was a two-week party. It brought out the best in our people, and the best in our athletes. We came fourth on the medal table, behind the US, Russia and China, which have nearly 2 billion people between them. So we did pretty good. Amazingly, the next time out, in Athens, we came fourth again. Hell of an effort.

SPORTING GREATS ACCORDING TO YOURS TRULY

We all have our own sporting stars, and we all share a few favourites like the amazing Don Bradman and Cathy Freeman. You can't not admire The Don or Our Cathy. Here are a few of my all-time greats.

Snowy Baker, The All-rounder

Snowy Baker was an incredible all-rounder. He excelled at almost all my favourite sports, being a champion swimmer and diver as well as a boxer. He played rugby union for New South Wales against Queensland, and then for Australia against Great Britain. At eighteen, he held the Australian middleweight and heavyweight boxing belts.

At the 1908 London Olympics, when we were in the one team with our Kiwi cousins, Snowy fronted up for Australasia in swimming and diving, and took a silver medal in boxing. Pretty good stuff! Baker was an early god in Australia. He could easily have been prime minister if he'd wanted to. Only had to say, 'Oh yeah, I'll have a go at that,' and the people would say, 'Fair enough, he's our man.'

Snowy Baker (left) with Duke Kahanamoku and Frank Beaurepaire.

Austin Robertson Snr, AFL Hall of Famer

I used to see quite a bit of Austin Robertson Jnr, who was also an AFL Hall of Famer and still holds the Western Australian record for the most goals kicked over his entire career. We'd meet at the cricket because he was involved with Kerry Packer and John Cornell in their World Series Cricket venture. And he used to tell me tales about his dad, Austin Robertson Snr, who had been a top AFL player too – and a champion sprinter. I became fascinated by his story.

In Melbourne in 1930, Austin Snr defeated the 'world sprint champion', Indigenous runner Lynch Cooper, and was awarded the world title. This caught the eye of Rupert 'Rufus' Naylor, who was a sports promoter and hustler, a sort of Australian Barnum or Bailey. He decided to take the new champion to America to compete in the big prize sprints over there. Austin Snr was actually at his best over about ninety yards, not a hundred, so in the middle of the night before one race, Naylor arranged for some blokes to sneak into the ground and shorten the track.

The big objective was a head-to-head race with US champion Eddie Tolan at the Chicago World's Fair. But for some reason Tolan had been unable to train and the race didn't happen. So instead, Naylor lined Austin Snr up against racehorses. And, of course, Austin Snr could beat a racehorse over fifty or sixty yards because a horse doesn't accelerate that quickly.

Don Bradman, Lord of Cricket

Bradman was the first name that I ever heard lorded in cricket, back when I was a very little kid. He was a god, the sort of god who could score 334 against what many still called the Old Country. I was about nine years old when he played his last test. He was in his twilight, but even in his twilight he could be the main weapon in thrashing our beloved enemy. No wonder you bowed your head when you said 'Don Bradman'.

The Don's career test batting average of 99.94 is one of the most famous stats in sport, so far ahead of the next best batsman that it was almost as if he was playing a different game. There are Bradman books and television shows and stamps and coins, and a whole lot of landmarks are named after him. But my favourite tribute is the way his average is commemorated in the address for the Australian Broadcasting Corporation. In every capital city, the mailing address for the ABC is Box 9994.

Cathy Freeman, Super Sprinter

There is a long tradition of female runners in Australia. But none has quite captured the hearts of Australians the way 'Our Cathy' did when she lit the Olympic flame in Sydney in 2000 then took out the gold medal in the 400-metres final. We loved her for that amazing effort, for her grace, her dignity and her cheeky smile.

I always smile when I see anyone Indigenous break out somewhere. Like the bowler Scott Boland, who turned up out of nowhere in our Ashes cricket team right at the end of 2021, then quietly took 6 for 7. It's such a relief to know they've survived everything they've had thrown at them and have managed to thrive. I'm proud of Cathy Freeman and Scott Boland, and so many others.

Johnny Devitt, King of Granville Pool

We have produced so many great swimmers: the Konrads Kids (brother and sister John and Ilsa Konrads), Murray Rose, Shane Gould, Ian Thorpe, Dawn Fraser, Leisel Jones, Susie O'Neill, Grant Hackett, Emma McKeon and on and on. It's something we do really well for such a lightly populated country, mainly because about 90 percent of the population lives within public transport range of a beach.

We've had so many world champions and still churn them out. But I'm going to nominate Johnny Devitt as my pick of them all because, well, there's a very personal connection. He's a couple of years older than me and went to my school, and he'd be doing his swimming training at the Granville pool while I practised my diving. Johnny won silver in the 100 metres at the Melbourne Olympics and a gold in the 4 x 200 metres relay. Then he won an individual gold in the 100 metres in Rome.

So he was the fastest swimmer in the world. Straight after Rome he married my sister, Wendy, at the St Oliver Plunkett's Catholic Church at Harris Park. So we gained an Olympic champion in the family. And not just that, but the most modest, straightforward, lovely bloke you'll ever meet. A class act. After his swimming career, he went to work for Speedo.

Sport was amateur then, and there was something nice about it being done for the love of it rather than for the money. The amount of moolah sports people make now is just absurd; back in the day, garbos and doctors played footy side by side for the love of the game. I look at basketball players' salaries and think, *As long as your kid's six foot seven, he's got a chance to make $50 million a year.* Anyway, the Granville Swimming Centre, where I worked as a pool attendant, and where Johnny and I both trained all those years ago, now has a John Devitt Pool.

Ken Thornett, Mayor of Parramatta

The Parramatta Eels were the closest first-grade rugby league team to Granville, so I was an Eels supporter. And the team's biggest stars were the Thornett brothers, particularly Ken. He was known as the 'Mayor of Parramatta' for his feats on the footy field, and if he had decided he wanted to be the real mayor of Parramatta I reckon he would have got 100 percent of the vote. He was captain and coach of the Eels in the mid-1960s and played full-back for Australia.

His brother Dick was an Olympic water polo player and represented his country in rugby union before joining Ken in rugby league at the Parramatta Eels. Dick also played rugby league for Australia. Their brother John was the captain of the Wallabies, the national rugby union team. Some family!

Lionel Rose, The Singing Boxer

Lionel Rose, a bantamweight, was the first Indigenous Australian to win a world boxing title. The whole country stopped to watch him take on the Japanese champion Masahiko 'Fighting' Harada in 1968. When Rose won, ten thousand people turned up at a public reception at Melbourne Town Hall. Lionel had a singing career too, but as a singer he was a wonderful boxer.

There have been so many great Indigenous fighters. I looked up to the Sands brothers when I was a teenager and was really into boxing. Dave Sands won fights in Australia, England and the United States. He had five brothers and they were all real top boxers too.

Rod Laver, Grand Slam Left-Hander

If there was any sport Australia dominated nearly as much as swimming, it was tennis. Through the 1960s and 1970s, particularly, we were on top of the world with Rod Laver, Margaret Court, Ken Rosewall, John Newcombe, Evonne Goolagong Cawley and many more. And we've had plenty of great players since, from Pat Rafter and Lleyton Hewitt through to recent women's world number one Ashleigh Barty. But Rod Laver is the one I most admire. For years this gritty left-hander was virtually unbeatable: he won 198 singles titles, on every surface, and eleven singles Grand Slams. He was ranked world number one for most of the 1960s, and helped Australia win four consecutive Davis Cups. You could fill this book just with his records.

I once spoke at a charity lunch that the then tourism minister, John Brown, organised. I was bullshitting about all the people I'd helped in little ways ('John Newcombe couldn't get on to women, so I told him, "John, grow a moustache."'), and I made a joke about Rod Laver. 'I met him as a young man,' I told the room, 'and he said he was going to give up tennis. It was too easy. He was bored with beating everyone so effortlessly. And I said, "Rod, here's an idea: try playing left-handed."' The reality, though, was that I didn't meet him as a young man, or at any time soon after that, in fact not until I took my first flight after the Covid pandemic. He was in the next seat and we started talking. He was everything I knew he would be: modest, friendly, quietly spoken; just a good, regular bloke. And I had to smile when he said, 'Brownie told me your joke about playing left-handed. Loved it.'

Ash Barty, Tennis Icon (and a pretty good cricketer too)

I preferred watching Ash Barty – another proud First Nations woman – to watching any of our men's tennis players from the modern era. Aside from her being such an admirable human being, she would win with technical skill and finesse rather than raw power. The rallies could go forever and you couldn't help but admire how she placed the ball. She was number one in the world until she decided to hang up the racquet. The fact she left tennis on her own terms made us admire her even more. And did I mention that when she decided to have a go at cricket, she proved pretty terrific at that too? Oh, and golf.

Our female sports stars have often carried us on the world stage. When we first had the Olympic Games down here, it was the women who were doing most of the winning. There have been times in Australia when I've flicked through the channels and seen women playing test-match cricket, AFL, soccer and rugby sevens. All on at the one time, and played with great passion and followed with equal passion. Not sure I've seen women's sport covered to that level in any other country.

Steven Bradbury, The Ultimate Underdog

Steven Bradbury was the short-track speed skater who became the first Australian, and the first person from the southern hemisphere to win a gold medal in the Winter Olympics. That's remarkable enough. Dorothea Mackellar said something about Australia being a land of ragged mountains. But we don't have mountains. We have hills. Nice hills, but hills all the same, to go with our sweeping plains and droughts and flooding rains. And across this whole great big continent it snows for about a month a year and covers not much more than a few acres. Our snow tends to be sparse and our ski runs are, sort of, snow ... ice ... snow ... rocks ... snow ... grass. So, if you can ski in Australia, you can ski anywhere in the world, and we do manage to send a team to the Winter Olympics and win medals.

But back to Bradbury and speed skating. He won his heat in the 1000 metres at the 2002 Olympics in Salt Lake City, and made it into the quarter-finals, where he finished behind the favourite and the reigning world champion – who was then disqualified over some technical infringement. So Bradbury sneaked into the semis, where, remarkably, all three competitors ahead of him crashed out. Then, in the final, he was running last – like, absolutely stone motherless last – with one corner to go, and with the four up front simply miles ahead and pushing each other really hard. So hard, they all collided and slid off the track. And our boy came sailing through to take the gold. Yeah, he was lucky, and it looks a bit like he's said, *Yeah, I'll have a go at this*, and somehow he's won it. But he had to be good to even get there, and he'd been training for years – he was the oldest guy in the final – and he'd refused to give up. What a hero, the ultimate underdog.

CHAPTER 4

How to Speak 'Strayan

A quick guide to being understood Down Under

I believe Australians have the most colourful, the most inventive and the slangiest version of English in the world. It's got a lot to do with how our country was started. We come from very humble beginnings, but we don't always like being humble, and our language reflects that.

Most of the convicts who were sent here to do time were lower-class English, so Cockneys were well represented in their number. They brought with them their rhyming slang, which they'd started using so that people in authority didn't know what they were talking about.

With rhyming slang, the trick was usually to know the whole expression, but drop the word that rhymed. There are hundreds of examples. Kids are *billies*, as in billy lid, the lid you'd put on your teapot. When you're on your own, you're *on your Pat*, which is a tribute to some mysterious man named Pat Malone. A suit's a *bag of fruit*. So for Australians, it's a *bagger*. Going down the road is *going down the frog and toad*. That becomes *the frog*.

Other expressions have nothing to do with rhyming slang. They come from all over the place, including the furthest parts of the outback. We adapt the sayings that are useful to us, or that we just like, in the same way we have adapted, and in some cases improved on, the world's food and coffee and everything else.

A lot of the old slang has disappeared from everyday conversation, partly as a result of us becoming the most diverse, most integrated country on the face of the earth. But it still comes out now and then. And certain expressions disappear for a few years, then suddenly everyone's using them again.

Proper Poms

Something I find really interesting is how Australian English varies so little from coast to coast. We sound much the same right across the continent. There are tiny regional variations, sure, but most people can't pick them. Any other place this size would be filled with accents. The Originals had 250 languages and 800 dialects before Europeans arrived. And now? One bloody language, one bloody accent.

When I was a kid, there was an exception to this one-accent rule though – and that was on radio and television. The first people on the idiot box, particularly the news anchors, had to speak in what was the closest they could get to Oxbridge English, or whatever you call it. Even Don Bradman, when he was being interviewed, put on a sort of posh voice. When you were talking on TV, you had to speak slowly and carefully in rounded tones. However, if you were on the telly or radio from the 1960s onwards, when stations began aiming at young listeners, you had to lean towards an American accent.

What you didn't hear, or see, on the airwaves, even then, was what you heard and saw everywhere else: Australians talking with broad Australian accents. Comedians back in the day were all Pommy guys who'd tell mother-in-law jokes. There we were, a country that loved a laugh and we were having to watch a bunch of Poms, usually the ones who weren't quite good enough to make it back home.

We were embarrassed about being Australian. We loved Bob Menzies when he was prime minister because he was always polite to the Queen, and because he enunciated so well. He was never going to embarrass us in front of Lizzy. Most politicians tried to follow suit, adopting the sort of embarrassing English that even the English didn't speak.

But then we slowly started getting this influence from television. It became the major social instructor in Australia, and we gradually became a little more American than English, or perhaps somewhere in between. The cultural cringe was still a thing, though, and Australians remained ashamed of their own accent. Even in the late 1960s, the idea of having someone who spoke like Bob Hawke running the government was as unthinkable as having a bloke like me on television. And when I advertised Winfield cigarettes in the early 1970s, it caused an uproar, not because I was selling a deadly product (for which I am eternally guilt-ridden), but because of the way I spoke. People were embarrassed to hear someone talking exactly the way a normal working-class Australian would speak.

When I was in London for the first time, I heard two girls talking in a bar, in this clean, correct, copybook sort of English. I knew straight away they were Australians. In tiny little England, the accents change with every street. They go from the Hooray Henrys through to Cockneys and Geordies that you can hardly understand. So the only people in England who spoke the sort of English these girls were speaking were Australians putting it on. And in those days, it was especially the girls, because, fair enough, they didn't want to sound like they were yobbos from Down Under.

Once back home, we often go out of our way not to speak proper English. I can't honestly explain why that is. I suspect it's part of our struggle for identity. I suspect it's also because we are different. We're not copying anyone, we do it our own way, which is playful and informal. The way we use language says: *I'm not going take you too seriously and I'm not going to let you take yourself too seriously.*

A dinkum dictionary

If you want to speak 'Strayan, you might want to bone up on the terms listed below. As well, you'll find other useful turns of phrase sprinkled throughout this book.

Accadacca How Aussies refer to one of my favourite Australian bands, AC/DC.

ambos These are the ambulance men and women. They are always voted the most respected workers of all, and it's not hard to see why. *Ambo* is one of the many words we've shortened and then added an 'o' to the end of. We'd never say, 'The garbage man's coming this afternoon.' No, 'The *garbo*'s coming this *arvo*.' There's *smoko, bottle-o, servo* – the list goes on.

Aussie salute Waving your hand to brush the flies away. There's no way to avoid it in summer. Even Prince Charles, when he's out here, has to do the *Aussie salute*.

bag of fruit A suit. If a bloke says he's going to *throw on his best bagger*, you know exactly what he's talking about.

bail To cancel plans. Often at the last minute. 'Kevin bailed' means Kevin isn't going to show up, or Kevin has shot through.

A long way to the top. You could have got pretty good odds against these blokes conquering the world, but they did it.

barbie That great Aussie institution, the barbecue. This is a word we shorten and add an 'ie' or 'y' to. Again there are countless examples: *brekkie* (breakfast), *brickie* (a bricklayer), *chippie* (a carpenter), *sickie* (a day off work sick), *bookie* (a bookmaker), *pollie* (a politician) and *footy* (which might mean rugby league or union, or Australian Rules football, depending on where you live). Even Christmas is *Chrissie*. Edna Everage once said, 'My husband's crook, he's in the *hozzie*.' But back to the *barbie*. We are the most barbecuey people on earth. It's partly the weather, it's partly the abundance of good meat, and it's partly that it's a very relaxed, informal way of having a meal. But there are rules. Traditionally, the man does the cooking outdoors. That was true even back in the days when, if a man was caught cooking a meal, people would ask, 'What's wrong with your missus?' The barbie was always the exception. After all, there was fire involved, so it was a bit dangerous and you didn't want the 'little woman' getting burnt out there. And there was no apron-wearing, so there was no shame in the man being the cook. The rules still apply. Including that the man does not do the cleaning afterwards. He shouldn't have to. He's just cooked you a meal!

better than a poke in the eye with a sharp stick It's good. How good? *Better than a poke in the eye with a sharp stick*. Some people say a *blunt* stick or *burnt* stick. Means the same.

beyond the black stump In the middle of nowhere. Comes from the idea of a black stump that marks the edge of civilisation. Beyond it is the outback.

Many people don't go beyond the Black Stump. Instead, they stop when they get to this delightful little pub in Merriwagga, NSW, which has the tallest bar in the southern hemisphere, according to publican Sharon Stuart. Merriwagga is one of several places that claim to be the home of the original black stump. It boasts a plaque unveiled by flamboyant pollie Al Grassby in 1970 that tried to make it official.

big-note To exaggerate your station in life, overstate your importance, wealth or success. When it comes to people big-noting themselves, I always think of Reg, the ganger, or boss, of the road crew I worked on while still a teen. Reg was much older, sixty or something, and although we'd all wear dirty old overalls to keep the hot liquid tar off our skin, not Reg. For him it was stubbies shorts and a T-shirt, mainly to show that he wasn't one of the workers. He was the ganger. He was the big boss! Whenever we'd pull up for a job, if there were members of the public around, he'd always talk a bit louder, ordering us all about – 'You get that over there, hurry up!' – so that the spectators knew Reg was important. One day we had a pretty big divot to fix next to a crowded bus stop. Reg squatted down to explain in his loudest voice how 'his' workers had to line up the diamond-tooth saw. And, when he got to his lowest position and held out his hand to show the exact line he needed, his cods dropped out of his shorts. None of us said anything. We all kept a straight face as he was squatting down there with his balls hanging out one side of his stubbies, going on and on, 'Take from the left side, move the marker up here, blah, blah, blah.' Reg assumed the people waiting for their bus were looking at him with wide eyes because he was important, because he was the ganger, the big boss. Maybe they were, but I'm pretty sure it was the other thing grabbing their attention.

billy A *billy*, or *billy can* is what you make tea in. But *the billies* are the kids, as in *billy lids*. Another one traced back to rhyming slang.

bloody oath Absolutely! 'Do you want another cold one?'… 'Bloody oath!'

bobby-dazzler Something truly terrific is *a real bobby-dazzler*. According to one definition, it's a phrase from the Geordie dialect, from the north-east of England, meaning a person who is considered (with affection) remarkable or excellent, shows smart dress sense or is 'flashy'. Maybe the term came from England but, like so many expressions, we've made it our own. And we don't use it for people, but for things.

bogan The Yanks have rednecks and hillbillies, we have *bogans*. This word wasn't around at all when I was young, but it gets a pretty good workout these days. The 2016 edition of the *Australian National Dictionary* defines it as 'an uncultured and unsophisticated person; a boorish and uncouth person'.

bonza Great. Terrific. It's an exclamation or an adjective: you can shout *'Bonza!'* in joy, or can have a bonza meal, or put in a bonza effort at the crease in the cricket final.

boofhead A stupid person is a real *boofhead*. It was the name of a character in a comic strip when I was really young, and the term has served me well ever since.

bottle-o Aka the bottle shop, the place where you buy your booze. Or, in the old days, a bloke who collected your empty bottles.

brasco A lot of old slang talkers, like my mate Lee Dillow, use this term for the toilet, as in 'I'm going to the brasco.' I was told 'Brass Co.' was once a toilet manufacturer, though the way Lee and others pronounced it, it rhymed with fiasco. Lee was a real blast of the old time in the way he talked. He came with us to the States as a roadie/acting representative, and when I moved over there and my business partner John Cornell came back, Lee stayed on. The Yanks loved him, because he spoke with such colourful slang; they'd just sit there and listen to him, like he was a poet. Which I guess Lee was.

William Buckley was an escaped convict who lived with the Indigenous Wathaurong people for thirty-two years. Some say his story inspired the saying Buckley's chance. He was still hoping to marry a supermodel when this rather fetching portrait was taken.

Buckley's chance   Little chance to no chance. 'Bill thinks he's going to one day marry Elle Macpherson, but he's got Buckley's.'

bugger   Buggery in some parts of the world is a sex crime. Here it's adapted into a term of affection: 'He's a funny bugger', 'He's a friendly bugger.' It's the same with *bastard*. Even calling someone *a crazy bastard* isn't a complete insult. Can be praise. It's all part of being Australian, where we can call complete strangers *mate*, and close mates *buggers* and *bastards*. No offence meant, none taken. 'Gee, you're a funny bastard!'

cactus   Dead, broken. 'I gotta get a new bike, the old one's cactus.'

chockers   'It's full to the brim. Can't fit another thing in. Completely chockers.'

chrome dome If you have a bald head, you're a *chrome dome*.

chuck a U–ie/U–ey When driving, you *chuck* a U-turn. However, you *throw* a right turn, and *hang* a left. You just do.

chuck a wobbly To have a maddy, to lose it completely.

chunder We have the biggest, and most colourful, collection of words for bodily functions. Let's not go too deeply into the grossest examples. Let's concentrate on what, in other countries, they call throwing up, or vomiting. Or, if they want to get slangy, hurling. In Australia you *chunder*, or *go for the big spit*, or the *technicolour yawn*, or a *rainbow yodel*. You *shout to Herb on the white telephone*. Why? Because 'Hhherbbb' is the noise you make while holding the outer rim of the toilet. My favourite is *driving the porcelain bus*. That's hard to beat; whoever thought up that one deserves a medal for cultural enrichment. Then there's *talking on the big telephone to God* ('Oohh!! God!!'). The Australian singer Jimmy Little had a hit song with the lyric 'You may talk to Jesus on this royal telephone', which we laughed at, but he was quite serious. He was talking about religion, not vomiting.

ciggie Also a *durrie*, a *dart*, a *coffin nail*. If you are visiting America or talking to Americans, do not ask if you can *bum a fag*. We never want to be offensive, so this is the kind of thing you have to watch out for.

clobber Your *clobber* is your clothing. When I was married and doing manual jobs, my side of the wardrobe contained a few singlets, a couple of sleeveless shirts and a few pairs of stubbies. That was the building worker's uniform. Didn't have a suit, just a pair of 'slacks' and one 'sports coat', which I'd wear to weddings and funerals. There were plenty of the former. All my mates got married about the same time. As many remarked, I didn't sharpen up my clobber much over the years. When we were over in the US in the mid-1980s doing the American edit of *Dundee*, we rented a house for the crew and it turned out to belong to Joan Collins. Joan came out on the first day, supposedly to show us her beautiful house, but probably to check out what undesirable riffraff had rented it. She was dressed and made up to the nines, and very pleasant. She apologised for the large number of pictures of herself that were scattered through the house.

END
GAMES

If a word's long, Australians shorten it. If it's short, we lengthen it by adding an extra vowel at the end. If your name's Smith, you're going to be *Smithy*. The most famous Smithy was Charles Kingsford Smith. He died shortly before I was born, but his legend remained and he became an airport. In the 1940s and early 1950s aeroplanes were rare enough that I'd yell to my younger brother, 'Quick, quick, out in the backyard. There's a plane going over.' And Pat'd come running.

It wasn't a large number of pictures, it was an enormous number. There were hundreds and hundreds of shots of her: magazine covers, glamour shots and the like. There were some with previous husbands in them, and, rather than take them down, she'd whacked stickers over the offending faces. Joan looked really good, and I said something to the effect that she looked like a million dollars, and Lee Dillow – our mate, roadie and Mr Fixit – said she just about melted. I bagsed Joan's bed, which was a big pink number with a heart-shaped padded pink headboard. Soon after we arrived, I had an afternoon nap on it, and Lee went and got John Cornell and Peter Faiman. They sneaked in to have a look and take a photo. I was wearing my black singlet and my black stubbies, and completely out to the world on this huge pink bed with its pink heart at one end. Lee said it was like a mud-soaked old blue heeler had come into the bedroom and jumped up on Joan Collins's bed. I just thought of it as two cultures colliding.

cooking with gas Everything's okay. 'Yep, you're cooking with gas.'

country mile In British English, a *country mile* is like a normal mile, only a great deal longer. The term is used a lot here because the joint is so big. Australians, on a per-capita basis, are the biggest international travellers in the world, and they tend to crisscross their own country too. But even after millennia of us populating the place, you can drive for hours and not see anyone. There are places in Australia you can walk where no human has ever been. You just go out in the middle of nowhere, stop your car and walk across open land. You can be pretty sure you're the first human to ever walk there. Can't say that about many countries. We are now 27 million. It was just seven million when I was born. Hell of a big country for seven million. So how big must it have been for our First Nations people?

crack the shits Getting angry at someone or something, often irrationally. 'I got him out first ball and he cracked the shits.'

crikey This was a gentler way of saying 'Christ!' I heard it all the time growing up. And then heard it all over America because it was Steve Irwin's catchcry. Irwin wasn't putting that on. That's how he talked. And – *crikey!* – his capers with dangerous animals did make for some exciting television.

crook *Crook* is a great word. When you're not talking about criminals, it means bad, or unwell. After a bad meal, you can be *as crook as a dog*, or *as crook as Rookwood*. Rookwood is a big cemetery in Sydney, so if you're as crook as Rookwood, you're as crook as you can be.

dag Someone who's a bit of a nerd or geek. The term is often used with affection. 'He's such a dag!'

damage I like that Australians call the restaurant bill or the price tag *the damage*. 'What's the damage, mate?'

dog's breakfast Originally it meant a piss and a look around the yard. Which can also be called a *swaggy's* (or *swagman's*) *breakfast* or an *eagle's breakfast*. Now the phrase is more often used to describe something very untidy, like a teenager's bedroom.

doing your 'nana Getting very angry. It's short for *doing your banana*, which is similar to *doing your block*.

don't come the raw prawn with me Don't try to put one over on me. I don't know whether this term comes from trying to trick someone into eating a raw prawn in order to make them sick, but I remember the era when people said it all the time.

don't get your knickers in a knot 'Don't get yourself angry and upset. Calm down, mate. It's all fine, we'll handle it. It'll be okay.'

drongo A great Australian word you don't hear often enough, particularly with so many *drongos* around nowadays. A drongo is a clot. A drip. A boofhead.

fair crack of the whip Or as the TV host Graham Kennedy used to say, 'fair suck of the sav', as in saveloy sausage. It means giving someone a fair go (see below). Former prime minister Kevin Rudd's version was *fair shake of the sauce bottle*, supposedly a Queensland variation. Norman Gunston – alter ego of Australian actor Garry McDonald – asked for 'a fair slice of the pineapple doughnut'.

fair dinkum Something that is *fair dinkum* is genuine, true, solid, authentic, ridgy-didge or dinky-di. You still hear this term, but not as much as you did. Sometimes it's just *dinkum*, which often means 'I'm not telling you any lies.'

THE
FAIR GO

What is the single greatest Australian expression? I nominate *the fair go*. The word *fair* is everywhere in this country, even in the title and chorus of our national anthem, 'Advance Australia Fair'. A fair go is an equal chance, and we reckon everyone has a right to that. It goes back to the convicts: what's fair and what isn't fair are so very important. You don't get that anywhere else in the world. Not in quite the same way.

This 1934 watercolour by Harold Herbert shows the facade of Melbourne's Myer Emporium, which gave rise to the expression more front that Myer's. The building was near another shop called Buckley & Nunn, which some believe gave us the term Buckley's chance.

front *Front* is nerve, or hide. It can be a good or bad thing. Someone with *plenty of front* could be a conman, claiming that he owns the Harbour Bridge and can sell it to you at a very special price. Or it could be some fearless rooster who steps up and asks tough questions of powerful people. Someone who has *more front than Mark Foy's* has a lot of front indeed. Mark Foy's was a department store in Sydney with a massive façade modelled on some big Parisian emporium (it's now the Downing Street court complex). It was on a corner facing Liverpool Street, and the building was so long it seemed to disappear into the distance along Elizabeth Street. In Melbourne it's *more front than Myer's*.

god–botherers People who come around to your door preaching.

grouse To complain. To have a whinge and a whine.

have a lend of someone To tease. If someone tells you a porkie (pie), and you believe them, they are successfully *having a lend of you*.

hoof it If you have to walk somewhere, you're *hoofing it*, or *travelling by shanks's pony*, a reference to using your shanks, or legs.

iffy When things are *a bit iffy*, they are questionable. A piece of meat that's been out of the fridge too long is a bit iffy. A raw prawn too.

knackered You go to the knackery to get spayed, to be neutered. Or to be boiled down for glue. 'I'm knackered' (or 'buggered' or 'rooted') is an entirely acceptable, widely used figure of speech to describe a state of exhaustion.

laughing gear Your *laughing gear* is your mouth, also known as your *cake-hole* or *pie-hole*. When someone offers you something worth putting into it, like a meat pie with sauce, or an ice-cold beer, they might say, 'Wrap your laughing gear around this.' There was a famous television ad for an ice cream, with a jingle that went, 'Wrap your laughing gear around a Paul's Billabong.'

melon Your head, otherwise known as your *noggin* or *bonce*. My melon got a pretty tough time when I was trying to make it in boxing. I was at work on the Bridge one Monday, nursing a cut that I had received on the weekend from a supposedly accidental headbutt during a bout. As I was working a crank handle to move a platform along, the handle flicked back and hit me on the forehead, opening up the cut. There was a bloke we worked with called Doc. We called him that because he was the nominated first-aid man, rather than because he knew anything whatsoever about medicine. I was sent to see him. Doc said, 'Come and sit here,' then looked up at my melon, and fainted.

mongrel A *mongrel* is a particularly unlikeable person. It's not a positive term, not like bugger or bastard. However, when someone isn't a mongrel, but has plenty of mongrel in them, that's a good thing. They are going to give it everything. You want them on your footy team.

mozzie A mosquito. Another example of abbreviating then adding 'ie'. Poker machines are *pokies*, sunglasses are *sunnies* and so on. One of my favourites is the charity known as Saint Vincent de Paul, which sells second-hand goods. If you ask, 'Where did you get the bagger, mate?', everyone knows what you're talking about when the answer is 'At Vinnies, of course.'

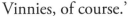

Hexham on the Hunter River in NSW is the home of 'Hexham greys', giant mangrove mosquitoes that can just about carry away small children. Being Aussies, we celebrate mozzies, and this is Aussie the Mozzie at the local bowlo.

no worries Another one of those Australian expressions that sums up a whole attitude, in this case our laid-back approach to everything. The Americans say 'no problemo' but that doesn't really have the same clout. When I started on television, doing little reports on *A Current Affair*, I'd never have a script. I'd just stand in the yard at Channel 9 and start talking at Greg Hunter, the cameraman. Greg was brilliant as a cameraman, but also brilliant as my one-man audience. Instead of looking at the camera, I'd be watching him. If I saw him let go with a smile or a contained laugh, I'd know Greg thought it was funny, and he was a pretty good judge. But that was a lot of pressure on Greg. Anyway, Greg wouldn't say 'no worries', he'd say 'no River Murrays', which became 'No rivers, I'll sort it out, mate'. He was full of that sort of rhyming slang and, as a result, everyone called him 'Rivers'. *No wucken furries* is another variation. 'It'll all be sorted, mate, no wuckens.'

A WAY WITH NAMES

We like to play around with people's names too. Barry becomes *Bazza*, Garry becomes *Gazza* and Darrell's *Dazza*. Oh, and *Muzza* for Murray. If your parents called you any of those names, that's what you're going to get for the rest of your life. But it's affectionate. You don't call complete strangers Bazza, Gazza, Dazza or Muzza, of course. But if you're a mate, I don't have to call you by your normal name.

nuddy Naked, nude. Barefoot all over.

Pat Malone If you're alone, you are *on your Pat Malone*, which becomes *on your Pat*. No one knows who Pat Malone was, but you'd have to guess he was a Neville No Mates from the dim and distant past.

Phar Lap The horse was before my time (he won the 1930 Melbourne Cup), but the saying 'He's got a heart like Phar Lap' is still going strong. Phar Lap supposedly had the biggest heart of any racehorse. So when someone has a huge ticker, we think of him. We've always been a horse-racing nation – Melbourne Cup Day is a public holiday in Victoria, and we are probably the only nation that stops to watch a horse race.

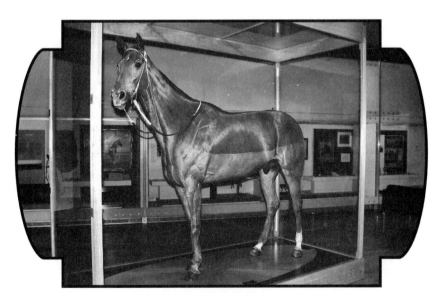

He lived just six years, but the mighty Phar Lap (1926–1932) was just what Australia needed for a bit of a cheer-up in the early years of the Depression. He's the only racehorse who was put out to pasture at the Melbourne Museum.

piss A common term for alcohol. You can be *on the piss*. Or you can *give up the piss*. And a *piss-up* is a big party. Everything's relative though. Drinking was a big part of blue-collar culture. Friday night would usually be pretty big and loud at the Harbour View Hotel. At some point my mate Bruce stopped turning up, and I was shocked when he announced, 'I've given up the piss.' He said that instead on Fridays he'd been getting the train straight back to Parramatta. 'I just drop into Dorrie's Hotel on the walk to the house, have four or five quick schooners and go straight home.' So that was Bruce's definition of giving up the piss, just four or five quick schooners, away from the boys. I would have been legless if I'd drunk that much that fast: that's nearly two litres of beer. Of course, on the weekend Bruce would also go to the club with the missus and give the neck oil a fair nudge there too. But as far as he was concerned, he'd changed his ways, turned a new leaf. He'd given up the piss.

pissed (off) The word *piss* is used a lot in the Aussie lexicon. To be *pissed-off* is to be annoyed at someone or something. The Americans see it differently, when they are angry, they are just pissed. If we're just pissed, we're somewhere between tipsy and legless.

pissing in someone's pocket When you are *pissing in someone's pocket*, you are flattering them. Therefore, when someone really does deserve a compliment, you have to make it clear you are not flattering them, because nobody likes a flatterer. 'I'm not pissing in your pocket, mate, but your new haircut looks half all right.' See also *take the piss*.

Pom An English person. We have a love–hate relationship with the Poms. We've always delighted in beating them in sport, but whenever they've had a scrape anywhere in the world, we've tended to rush over and fight for them. I've heard several explanations for the name, but the one I believe is that Poms were called *poms* because the convict uniforms used to have POHM – Prison of His/Her Majesty – written on them.

rack off A friendly way of telling someone to go away. Well, friendly compared with a lot of other terms Australians use to tell someone to go away.

Reg Grundies Undies, or underpants. Reg Grundy was a TV producer, and a lot of TV shows in the 1960s and 1970s would announce at the end, 'This has been a Reg Grundy Production.' That was the only thing most people knew

about Reg Grundy. Some of his shows were copied off US formats, but they were hits and he did well. Really well. When I was in the Bahamas in the mid-1990s, filming *Flipper*, the house I rented belonged to the actor Richard Harris, and the crown from *Camelot* came with it for no extra cost. Reg Grundy lived next door. It was on Paradise Island, which is not really an island – you just cross the bridge onto the mainland – but it's pretty spectacular. And he had this bloody big house and a beautiful big boat with Gordon Ramsay as his on-board chef. Reg Grundy died in 2016, at ninety-two, but he lives on in the language as *a pair of Reg Grundies*. He left his mark, so to speak.

rellies, rellos Short for relatives. This is a rare case where there is dispute about whether to put an 'ie' or 'o' at the end.

ridgy–didge All good. Correct. Straight down the line. The real deal.

right as rain Good, solid, dependable. In a parched, sunburnt country like ours, rain is something you look forward to. It's not always a positive for those living in the city or planning a trip to the beach, but in the country, if it's good, solid or dependable, they'll say it's *right as rain*. And they'll mean it literally.

ripper An expression of delight, as in 'You little ripper!' It might be directed at a person who's just done something great, or it might be yelled up at the heavens. Where does that come from? I don't know. Why was it a *little* ripper? Same answer. But it is a little ripper, and a little ripper is better than a full-sized one. Maybe it's another example of

Australian understatement: making it smaller emphasises how big it is. Or something.

root There are words that don't travel well, like *bum*, *fag* and *root*. You can't help laughing to yourself when you're in America and hear people using this word. They say they are rooting for the home team, and you wonder if it does the home team any good. For anyone who doesn't know, *root* is a much politer and very Australian way of saying the F-word. In America you see the plumbing trucks running around with 'Roto-Rooter' drain-clearing equipment onboard. Some have signwriting across them that says 'Mr Rooter' or even 'America's Best Rooter' – talk about having tickets on yourself. When I was young, the Lidcombe State Hospital, which was an old men's home, was widely known as the Dun Rooten. A lot of those men's places were called Dun-something (*dun* is Scottish for fort). So, of course, we thought if a bloke's gone in there, he's done rooting. There was no harm meant, and no one batted an eyelid.

rooted When used in the past tense, *root* has no sexual connotation. A runner at the end of a marathon is rooted. A car that has been hit by a semi-trailer is really, really rooted. A lightweight footballer who has been smashed by a prop with cauliflower ears is likely to be pretty rooted as well.

rubbidy–dub The pub. Of course.

servo A service station. Calling the pump a *bowser* is another term you hear only in Oz.

sheila A person of the female variety. Aka, in less enlightened times, the *little woman*, the *ball and chain* or, in the marriage game, the *trouble and strife* (wife). It was a long time before they became *the better half*. We do keep improving.

she's apples Everything's sweet, everything's ridgy-didge, you're cooking with gas. It's short for 'She's apples and spice', meaning she's nice.

shoot through To leave or depart, usually when you want to get out of a tricky situation.

shout Anywhere else in the world, to *shout* means to yell out. Here it also means taking your turn to buy a round of drinks, a noble Australian tradition. If you have friends, you have to shout or you'll get a reputation for having short arms and deep pockets. There's a ritual about whose shout it is, and if you go drinking with ten mates, it can be a problem because you might have to pay for – and drink – ten beers. Shouting is a part of kinship or mateship, and if you're with good mates, you don't need to keep count. But if you're not, you might need to because there are people who *wouldn't shout if a snake bit them*, or *wouldn't shout in a shark attack*, and they have all sorts of tricks to avoid buying a round, like holding the door open so that everyone gets to the bar before them, then suddenly disappearing when it's their turn.

sickie A *sickie* is a day off work because you are ill. However, if you *pull a sickie*, you are not really sick. You're probably at the cricket, or the beach, or the rubbidy-dub.

Smoko on the Bridge. The smoko still gives millions of Aussies a respite from hard manual labour – and a chance to spin a few yarns.

slab A carton of beer. A party in a cardboard box, something to grab from the bottle-o and carry home on your shoulder.

smoko The break you take on your work shift: a smoking break. The term's still used, even though we shouldn't be smoking.

sook If you always sulk or whinge about things, you're a *sook*. Nobody likes a sook.

spit the dummy To carry on like a baby having a tantrum – which is to say *spitting the dummy* out of the pram or across the room, while turning red with rage.

stickybeak If you are putting your nose into other people's business, or where it shouldn't be, you're a *stickybeak*. Everyone's mum told them *not* to be a stickybeak, to mind their own business.

stinker A stinking hot day is a *stinker*. There are various things that go with it, like getting in a car and having your fingers burnt by the seatbelt buckle. But you learn to love that, especially if you've ever been really cold. We whinge about the weather, but we don't have tornadoes, we don't generally have earthquakes, and we don't get a metre of snow, except in places where we want it. It's a great climate. We're not frozen to death, we don't really have heatwaves or monsoons. Sure, we had Cyclone Tracy and a few other batterings, but we don't have any places that get the endless misery of Tornado Alley in the States. Granville, and the west in general, was a pretty hot part of Sydney. But we didn't know any different. We didn't miss air-conditioning because we never had it. It's summertime, it's going to get hot, you just cop it. The compensations are pretty good: we're in a beautiful part of the world and most of us live near the beach and can get there fairly easily. When I worked on the top of the Bridge, it was pretty bloody hot. But you always had a breeze. Yeah, sometimes too much of a breeze, but I loved it up there.

When I worked on the top of the Bridge, it was pretty bloody hot. But you always had a breeze. Sometimes, too much of a breeze.

straight to the pool room When someone gives you a present that's really good, like much too good to ever be used, it's going *straight to the pool room* to be put on show. It's one of the many wonderful lines from the Australian film *The Castle* that have passed into the language.

strewth Short for 'God's truth'. An exclamation still used by older Australians.

swag A single bed you can roll up, a bit like a sleeping bag. The swagman, or travelling labourer, with all his possessions rolled up into his swag, is a mainstay of Australian bush tales. They weren't always jolly.

take the piss *Pulling someone's leg* is similar, but *taking the piss* is a much more typically Australian way of saying it. It can mean sending someone up or playing a practical joke on them. More politely, you can *take the Mickey* out of someone, which is generally cut back to *taking the Mick*. If you send someone up, it's a *piss-take*.

tell him he's dreamin' Meaning tell him his suggestion is ridiculous, it's never going to happen. Another one from *The Castle*, that most Australian of Australian movies. It's now studied as part of the school curriculum, and you hear sayings from it in normal conversation all the time: 'Ah, the serenity' … 'We're going to Bonnie Doon' … 'It's the vibe.' Another way of saying *Tell him he's dreamin'* is *he's having a lend of himself*.

thongs Another Aussie word that doesn't travel very well. We're talking here about Australian thongs – the Poms call them flip-flops – not the ones where your arse hangs out. Thongs are a significant part of our national wardrobe. It's a nice warm country and it's easy to slip these sandals on and off. You can see why they swept the country, because they're a piece of piss to put on, with no shoelaces to tie up. We *are* lazy.

tickets on her/himself   Someone with *tickets on themselves* is up themselves. Everyone knows such a person is a bit of an ego-tripper, has a big head. In other words, what a wanker!

top bloke   If you're a *top bloke*, it doesn't mean you're the boss or you're even in a senior position. No, being called a top bloke means you're a good man, a really good man. And strangely, in this case, there is no understatement, no irony. When we think something is really good we tend to say, 'It's not bad', but this is an unusual case where we actually say what we mean. A top bloke really is a top bloke.

tracky daks   Tracksuit pants, of course. The word *tracky* distinguishes them from other pants, which are also *daks*. As in, 'Put your daks on, and we'll go.'

trots   If you have diarrhoea, that's *the trots*. Another term tied in with horses, and proof that not all our colourful turns of phrase relating to bodily functions are about throwing up.

truckie   Another 'ie' word, denoting a man or woman who drives a truck. For a cab, it's a *cabbie*. A train driver isn't a trainie, though. That would be silly.

true-blue Genuine. It's a bit like *fair dinkum*, but with more emphasis on being Australian. The first Holden was a true-blue car, Qantas is a true-blue airline.

up yourself Stuck up. On very good terms with yourself. Having both feet planted firmly in mid-air.

Woop Woop A mythical town that is way out in the back of beyond, or, as we also say, *out in the boonies* (boondocks) or *beyond the black stump*. In *Crocodile Dundee* we had Walkabout Creek. Same difference.

youse The plural of you. It's heard around the world, but rarely uttered with the finesse of Australian boxing champion (and mate of mine) Jeff Fenech, after he won his 1987 title fight against Thailand's Samart Payakaroon. 'With twelve thousand of the most beautifullest people in the world cheering me on, it's hard to feel pain,' said Jeff, covered in blood and sweat and bruises. 'I love youse all.' And he did.

CHAPTER 5

All in the Family

'Wait until your father gets home'

Family life altered dramatically in the time when I was a teenager. We were coming out of an age of war, shortages and bleakness, into a world of television, rock 'n' roll and washing machines (you might be surprised what a big deal our first one of those was). Our country got its first Australian-made car too, the Holden, and we were delighted, even if it would be years and years before anyone in our family could afford one. On top of all that, we were being introduced to the best of the world as postwar immigration got into full swing. The momentous changes were a lot for our parents and grandparents to deal with, but us youngsters loved it.

House rules

Back when I was growing up, almost everyone lived in houses, each on their own quarter-acre block of land. Nobody lived

The Castle. The classic Australian postwar home was on its own quarter-acre block with a driveway, whether you could afford a car or not, and an outside dunny covered in choko vines.

in flats (apartments) or townhouses, except maybe a few city workers. And those city workers were usually bachelors, though very occasionally there might be a single girl or a lady in an inner-city flat. There was nothing sophisticated about apartment living as far as we knew. We felt sorry for them. 'Poor bastards, no backyard!' Because you lived in your backyard.

So what was a typical home in the suburbs like in the early 1950s, say, when I was entering my teens? I don't think they came much more typical than the ones where I lived, in Granville, in Sydney's Western Suburbs.

There were rows of houses, all much the same. You had a front gate and a bit of a front yard, and if you were posh you might decorate it with some statues of flamingos. In some other parts of the city I saw front yards with statues of Indigenous people with spears. Not in the west, though.

Not everyone had a car, but everyone had a driveway at the front. It would be off to one side of the house and with a separate gate. You had to have two gates at the front, you just did. The driveway would usually be two narrow strips of concrete leading to a garage or carport, if you were lucky enough to have one or the other. But sometimes it would be just twin dirt tracks leading to an open space.

Mod cons

All the houses I knew had three bedrooms. The one-storey, small square house was fairly normal in the Western Suburbs. They were never big enough. My brother and I shared a room. My sister had her own room. But if you happened to have seven kids, as did many of the families at our school, you'd still just as likely have three bedrooms.

The toilet was outside, but the bathroom was inside. It had an enamel bathtub with big feet on it, and running water. Australians always had baths; showering was an American thing that you'd see in the movies. The laundry was outside too. Clothes dryers were unknown, but my family was out of the blocks early in getting an electric washing machine. Dad was a purchasing officer for the army, and he used to be given all sorts of samples, and that somehow gave him the inside running on this strange machine.

It clamped onto the edge of the laundry tub. You'd put your washing and some soap into the tub and fill it up with hot water, which you'd heated in the copper, next to the tub. Then you'd throw your clothes or sheets in and lower the washing machine's rotor and turn it on. It would whip up the water, and foam up the soap, and supposedly get everything clean, though I seem

Technology was racing ahead so quickly in the 1950s that many of us were sure everything that could ever be invented already had been. A machine that could wash your clothes was enough to draw a crowd!

to remember it destroying almost as many things as it washed. And Mum still had to rinse everything and wring it at the end by running it by hand through a set of rollers, or mangle.

Still, all the neighbours came in to have a bit of a look. We felt pretty important, having a washing machine. Should have charged admission. It wasn't until maybe the late 1950s that ordinary people started getting proper washing machines, the type that did everything including the spin cycle.

Entertaining at home

In most houses, everything revolved around the kitchen and the dining room, a glassed-in back veranda that was like an annex to the kitchen. At the front, the living room was the flash part of the house, for sitting around listening to the radio and entertaining visitors. There was usually a glass-fronted cabinet in there, and that's where all the good stuff was. You know, the fancy crockery and the posh silver and other stuff that was kept 'for best', and only used when we had people over.

That said, my parents entertained quite a bit, because my dad had nine siblings. (They weren't Catholics, but they were Irish; it was my mother who was the Catholic, and she was an only child.) So there were often uncles and aunties coming over and all the grown-ups would be in that front room talking, and the kids would be out in the backyard having a cricket match or a game of footy.

Today there might be a barbecue, but our food was always cooked in the kitchen. Barbecuing wasn't that common in the 1940s and early 1950s. Nowadays, having a house without a barbie is almost illegal, but it just wasn't a thing back then.

Backyard business

Every decent house had a toolshed and an outdoor dunny behind it, with choko vines growing over both of them. Chokos are a vegetable, or maybe a fruit. Either way, it didn't matter, because you never ate them. No, you just threw them at each other. They were like hand grenades, exploding on impact. Why chokos on the dunny? No idea, but they were on every dunny in every backyard.

The toolshed held a few basic tools and a push mower. Which is to say a mower with no engine, just some blunt blades that tried to thrash the lawn into submission. And we had buffalo grass in the front, which was tough stuff, and, thrash as we might, the grass often won. This futile attempt at home maintenance was my job and I hated it.

I was really jealous of the man next door, Tom Maudsley, because he had a very early power mower. We're talking maybe the very late 1940s. The blades weren't rotary, they were in the shape of a drum like our push mower. The Maudsley contraption was powered by electricity, which sounds dangerous and was. He had to mow the lawn while carefully moving the cable, so the mower didn't run over it and cause everything to light up. We used to go and gawk at old Tom at work, constantly moving the cord and being forced to mow in strange patterns because he could only go so far before he ran out of power lead.

Us kids dreamt of having a machine that would do that. Amazing! *He must be rich*, we thought. But looking back, if he was living next door to us in Granville, I don't think he had an abundance of money. An old bloke one block over maybe had a better idea: he'd concreted over his front lawn altogether. I used to find myself gazing at it after school, full of envy for this front 'lawn' that never needed mowing.

Generally, though, there was a lot of garden pride on display at the front of people's houses. At the back, none. There was always a patch of dirt in the grass, which was the crease for a set of cricket stumps, and another patch with the grass worn away, which was the bowler's mark. There were also various sticks poking out of the ground to mark out the try

The backyard was the perfect setting for family photos. Here, my sons Clay and Todd give moral support to my eldest, Brett, on his first day of school. Noelene and I were still almost kids ourselves.

TO AND FROM
YOUR DOOR

The milkman usually had a horse and cart, and his horse would stop right in front of each house – we were amazed by such an intelligent animal. The milk didn't come in bottles. Instead, the milkman would fill up a jug we left in a box around the side of the house. In summer particularly, you'd always want to get the milk early or it would be more the consistency of yoghurt.

Drinks were kept cool in an icebox, and the iceman also used to come each day. The baker would deliver on his horse and cart as well, and the bottle-o would pick up your empties – everyone came to you in those days. We then saw the iceman's business melt away when we, like many others, bought an electric fridge later in the 1950s.

There was no sewerage in our Granville street. It was a 'cart-away', which meant the 'night-soil man' came and collected the waste from our toilet, or dunny. Of course his business card might have said 'night-soil man' but to us he was the 'dunny man' or 'Dan Dan', after a character in a popular radio serial. It can't have been the greatest job, walking around with a shit can on your shoulder, but at least the shit carters had a truck rather than a horse and cart. Same with the garbos, who'd hurl the contents of our circular metal bins into the back of their truck. Everything went into the bin: boxes, newspapers, glass jars, paint tins, the lot. No such thing as recycling. We never heard the term.

The only rubbish that didn't go into the bin (mainly food scraps and grass clippings) would go onto the compost heap, and the compost would then be put on the garden. We also had an incinerator next to the toolshed, and there was always someone burning something in that. We didn't know much about keeping the air clean, and I have strong memories of it billowing black smoke as we filled it with items we'd never consider burning today.

How to Speak 'STRAYAN

shitcan

The dunny man, or sewage collector, carried a shit can. Today, to *shitcan* something or someone is to say something bad about it/them.

ankle biters

Little kids are *ankle biters*. I had my ankles bitten really early. And late. And often. There're forty years between my oldest and youngest, and four children in between.

clucky

Feeling maternal.

lines or goals or safety zones, because you played football and soccer and chases and all that in the backyard too. As well as going to war armed with the aforementioned chokos.

The backyard was also where the clothesline was. Usually this was two posts with a cross arm and lines, or ropes, suspended between them. I can remember a guy used to come around with a horse and cart, yelling, 'Clothes prop, clothes prop.' He was selling these long sticks with a big vee on top of them. You pegged everything on your clothesline when it was low and used these sticks to prop it up high when you were finished. Then you removed the prop to get your washing down when it was dry. Otherwise your sheets and things were rubbing against the ground.

We got flash. We bought a Hills Hoist, a great Aussie invention. This height-adjustable, spinning clothesline likely put the poor clothes-prop man out of business.

We got flash. We bought a Hills Hoist, a great Aussie invention.

Our own set of wheels

We were as proud as anything when Australia finally manufactured a car: the 1948 Holden. I was young then, but I remember the excitement of seeing the prime minister, Ben Chifley, launching 'Australia's own car'. Until then, as far as we knew, only the French, Italians, Yanks and Poms had come out with their own cars. But now we had ours, to go with our own international airline, Qantas. It was like a reward for enduring all the hardships and austerity of the war. 'She's a beauty!' Chifley said as he saw the number-one Holden coming down the line.

The original Holden, the 48-215, was of far more interest to us than any politician, including Prime Minister Ben Chifley, seen here with car number one coming off the production line at Fishermans Bend in Melbourne.

Within about ten years, everyone had their own Holden. Everyone except me. I had to wait a long time – and for a football injury. It happened in the late sixties while playing with the Sydney Harbour Bridge rugby league team when I went for a head-high tackle. I was going to take this guy's melon off, but he dipped it at the wrong moment and headbutted my extended thumb, right on the end. My thumb went like a spear into the rest of my hand.

It hurt like hell, but, in the finest Australian tradition, I managed to nurse it all weekend and bundy on at the Bridge on Monday morning. That way, I could say I'd been injured at work. (The bundy clock, by the way, was the machine that you punched your card into at work. It proved you'd turned up, and recorded what time you arrived and left.) I was sent to hospital and got pretty well my whole lower arm put in plaster and was off on compo for a few weeks. The guys all felt sorry for me and had a whip-around. They raised about $300 and I spent it on my very first car. It was an old Holden, from 1950-something. It'd had a hard life and looked pretty ordinary, but a neighbour of mine spray-painted it black for £10. That would have scarcely paid for the paint, but he just liked doing it.

Trading up

So there I was, twenty-eight years old and finally the owner of my first four-wheeler. I could drive to work at last, and back then parking wasn't a problem. You could easily find a spot on the street, even right under the Bridge. When I started doing the little skits on television, my trusty Holden enabled me to drop into Channel 9 on my way home.

My right thumb still won't move all the way back, but I got my own set of wheels and a few weeks on the couch out of it. I bought two more Holdens second-hand after that one. Then, in the early 1970s, after I started flogging cigarettes and had more money than I ever needed, I bought a new one, a big silver Holden Statesman. Good thing. The Statesman, Kingswood, Torana and Commodore and all those other models are history now. But for nearly seventy years we had the Holden, our own Aussie car. We also made Fords and Toyotas and other things here too, but not anymore. That's a damn shame.

Parenting, 1950s–style

Australian fathers didn't participate much in family life when I was young, except when it came to dealing out punishment. The mothers did most of the child raising. It was still very much a Christian nation, and my mum was full of all the Christian clichés. You know, 'If you can't say something nice about someone, don't say anything.' And true to form, I never heard her say a bad word about anyone.

No idea how she managed that. She certainly could have been forgiven for saying a few bad words about me. I was a born larrikin (see Chapter 7), getting into all sorts of trouble. A bit light-fingered too. I'd nick stuff from the house, or from shops, anywhere. I put it down to my convict heritage.

I never heard my mum say a bad word about anyone. She certainly could have been forgiven for saying a few bad words about me.

The first Woolworths in our district was more like a cheap department store than the supermarket of today. I remember it well, because when I was six or seven I shoplifted a Woody Woodpecker whistle from there. It had a little pump on it and would make that cackling noise the cartoon character made. I was so dumb that I took it out of the packet and threw the wrapping on the ground right next to our front gate. (We weren't environmentally conscious in the 1940s, or even later, in the fifties and sixties. People tossed rubbish out of their car windows, threw the wrappings from takeaway food or other packages straight in the gutter. You didn't stop to think where it went afterwards, but that was the way it was.)

Soon I'd irritated everyone with my whistle.

'Where'd you get that from?' asked my mother.

'I got it off a friend,' I replied.

'Then what's this thing here?' she asked, holding up the incriminating packaging.

My good Catholic mother was horrified, but the only admonishment from her was, 'Wait until your father gets home.' He got home. And he belted me.

I've been trying to think of fond memories of my father. I don't have any, and that's really sad. He was in the army, which maybe made him more distant, and he was also of that generation that thought children should be seen and not heard. Fathers like my dad were never affectionate. That might have been a bit too sissy for them.

I don't know what changed, but my generation of dads were much more involved with their children. I love my kids and I'm close to all of them. And they are every bit as close, or even more so, to their own children.

Making your own fun

You didn't kick a ball with your dad in the 1940s or early 1950s. You didn't watch television with them either, because there wasn't any. You made your own entertainment. When I wasn't nicking stuff, I'd go with my mates down to the stormwater canal at Granville. This was a concrete creek with grass reserves on each side, right near our house. Leading into the canal were all these concrete pipes that carried water there after rain. Every so often a rat would stick its nose out of one of these pipes. To a ten-year-old boy, this was an open invitation.

My mum and dad didn't mind me going down to the canal to knock off rats. You were doing a public service.

All my mates had slingshots or catapults, and one of them who was rich had an air rifle. My mum and dad didn't mind me going down to the canal to knock off rats. You'd have wondered if they did: rats were known to carry diseases and they were pretty unattractive, so why would you even think twice about killing them? You were doing a public service. Still, although my parents were happy for me to serve the community in this way, they wouldn't let me have any weapons.

The rats were really big and we'd stand at the top of the canal to get a good view. As the unarmed member of the group, I could only throw stones, and I became a really good shot. It was like going on safari, going down to the stormwater canal. On a good day we might get three rats each. I became such a good shot that it inspired me to write the scene in *Crocodile Dundee* where Mick hurls a can over a crowd to brain a robber.

Problem child

The stormwater drain played a part in me breaking my first bone too. I was riding a pushbike down the nearby grassy hill, a hill that wasn't meant to be ridden down, as it was so steep it was nearly a cliff. But there were about five of us on pushbikes, and the other guys dared me to be the first to try it.

Dopey old me could never say no to a dare, a trait that surfaced again and again. So down I went – faster, faster, faster – and then, yep, the front wheel dug into the ground and I flew over the handlebars. My arm went straight out to protect my face, and I broke my elbow. But I'd done it: I'd risen to the challenge. Then, of course, I had to pretend it didn't hurt.

The parents were not impressed. Yet again. It wasn't till many years later that I stopped to wonder why I had always been shipped off to my aunties during the school holidays.

Four of them seemed to share me and I never went to the same one twice in a row, and my brother and sister never came with me. Only then did I realise that I'd been the problem child.

Still, my aunties were really great. They all lived around the Western Suburbs in streets like ours, except Auntie Coo and Uncle Ron, whose house was set among the cows and horses and market gardens in a place called Merrylands. It seemed a world away, but when I look at the map now, it was only a couple of miles west of our place. It would soon be pure suburbia.

School rules

Australian schools in the 1940s and 1950s taught us about the third wife of Henry VIII and that sort of stuff. It was all kings and queens, and English battles, but nothing to do with us. Or it was ancient history: the Egyptians or the Roman Empire. Our Indigenous peoples? Almost never a mention.

Was it Henry the Sixth who had eight wives, or the other way around? Maybe he had 1066 of them, and that's why he's looking a bit out of sorts here. School back in the day was all foreign facts and ancient dates that meant very little to us.

Me, big sister Wendy and little brother Pat, all dressed up to go to school. Wendy was the scholar. I'm sure Pat and I were already thinking about what we were going to do as soon as the day's school was over.

It was like there was no Australian history. Okay, you learnt a bit about Captain Cook and Admiral Phillip, but that was about it. Mind you, not a lot of it registered. I was too busy throwing stuff at other kids, or being the clown, or passing notes around about what we were going to do at playtime.

Even while doing all that, I was good at school early on. Then I lost interest, except in physics, which fascinated me. The other subjects were just something you had to do. I used to get particularly poor marks in English, because nobody could read my blotty, messy cursive. However, towards the end of school, I started putting humour into my essays and working a little bit harder on them, for no other reason than I was having fun. At first it didn't affect my marks, because no one could decipher my unholy scrawl. Then suddenly one of the English teachers cracked the code and gave me the best mark in the class. I can't remember what that essay was about, maybe because it didn't matter to me at the time. I could never have imagined that writing would be part of my career.

My appalling handwriting never did improve. I probably didn't want to learn to write well because I figured anyone who did would end up writing up the price tags and stickers at Woolies. And I never learnt to type because no male was taught to type when I was growing up. The idea was that if you did anything worthwhile workwise, you'd have a secretary and she'd type it out for you.

That's made writing emails difficult to this day. I can hunt and peck at best, so most of my emails contain just one sentence: 'I will call you.' I never used any written notes when I started doing television, just made it up as I went. When I started writing scripts that other people would need to understand, I wrote them in longhand in block capitals. I did my first emails in capitals too, but, after I'd been doing it for about a year, I discovered it means you're shouting.

Religious wars

In Australia there were Catholics and there were Protestants and that's all there was, as far as we knew. We were the Catholics – pronounced *kafalicks* – and the Protestants, who we called proddos, were the other side. It might sound like a recipe for violent struggle, but it never went beyond a bit of taunting.

My Marist Brothers school at Parramatta backed onto the King's School, which was really, really posh, and really, really proddo. They wore what looked like army uniforms, and the school had rolling green fields that disappeared into the distance.

We used to hurl verbal abuse over the fence, usually with insults that are definitely no longer PC. But it wasn't a big deal. The main conflict between kafalicks and proddos occurred when one had a holiday coming up that the other didn't get. I still remember them singing, 'Catholics have to go to school, Catholics have to go to school.'

A town divided

Schoolboys like us throwing insults and the odd pebble back and forth was harmless enough, but religion caused its fair share of real trouble in Australia. While not at the same levels as in places such as Northern Ireland, it still broke up families and relationships. My mate Bill, originally from north-east Victoria, was a classic case. Bill met the delightful Gloria in the late 1950s at an old-time dance in the little township of Tallangatta (population: about two hundred at the time). They quickly fell

The day of my First Communion. Christianity played a big part in everyone's life back then. But television, rock 'n' roll and more blow-ins were on the way, and everything was about to be turned on its head.

in love and started making grand plans. The obvious problem though was that Bill was Catholic and Gloria was Protestant.

Gloria's parents barred her from seeing Bill and suddenly this quiet little farming community was split down the middle. Now Bill lived about sixteen miles away from the little township but, like in any great love story, this didn't deter either of them and they took every opportunity to meet up, though it could only ever be briefly. You see, the local copper was also Protestant and as soon as Bill was seen in his old cattle truck heading for the township by anyone in the congregation, they'd be on the phone to the copper and he'd rush to Gloria and make sure she was 'safe' until Bill had left town.

This resulted in Bill borrowing vehicles from other Catholics, wearing wigs and even at times riding a horse for twenty miles through the bush. In the end no one could stop Bill and Gloria being together and they planned to get married. But Gloria's family disowned her and not one family member attended the wedding, not even her brother or her sister who she had been incredibly close to. Nine years later, when Bill and Gloria's first child was born, her parents sheepishly reconnected with the family and they had a great relationship from there on, particularly with Bill, who, once they got to know him, they found was a top bloke.

The final silly thing about all this is that Gloria's family weren't even religious. They were lapsed Protestants, didn't go to church, and didn't even have a Bible in the house. All they were worried about was what other people would think if their daughter married a Catholic. As a result of such foolishness, they wasted many years they could have been spending with their daughter. Such stories were all too common at the time.

Believe it ... or not

These rivalries have almost disappeared today, as religions have declined. I guess it's called reality. Mum was a devout Catholic. At the age of 101, she had a good breakfast and went and laid down and died, believing she was off to heaven. Wow.

So I've never sneered at or derided religious people, even in a world where I've learnt there are a lot more flavours than Catholic and Protestant. I envy the devout: I love that thought that, *Well, I'm a good person, so I'll go to heaven.* What a way to go out. I wish I could believe that.

Mum made my dad become a Catholic, and we children had a religious education. I did the altar boy thing and made my first communion and all that, for my mum's sake. And we all went to church, for a while at least. I'm pretty sure I was married in a Catholic church too. Though I don't really remember the wedding, as I was only a teenager.

Plenty of claims are made for religion, but I haven't seen a lot of evidence of it bringing people together.

Work in the land of opportunity

It was normal to get out of school at fifteen and get a job. Only the boffins stayed on another two years and got their leaving certificate, and there weren't many boffins back then. There was plenty of work around. At Flemington, at what's now part of the Olympic site, there was a big abattoir. Half of my mates worked there. They used to hire day workers, so guys who were between jobs, or had never had a full-time job, used to go to the 'abs' and work on the boning table or as a brain sorter.

hard yakka

Hard work is *hard yakka*. Yakka derives from *yaga*, meaning work in the Yagara language of the Brisbane region. It later became a brand name for tradie clothing.

Just occasionally a few super-boffins would go on to uni. I remember only one in our whole year, Eddie, who wanted to be a doctor. My sister got her leaving certificate, which was unusual, but there weren't that many opportunities for smart women back then, so she didn't go to uni.

If Eddie and my sister were exceptions, my brother, Pat, and I were the rule. We left school the moment we could and went to work. We were still on the old currency when I got my first job. It was 1954 and I was an apprentice moulder. The basic wage was about £14 a week. A first-year apprentice got three and a bit pounds, and it went up to £5 or so in your second year. I got the job because a neighbourhood family, the McKelveys, owned an iron foundry. Johnny McKelvey was a mate of mine and I went to work there with him.

A hard body and a lot of blackheads caused by the filthy air, that's all I got out of being in the foundry. Because I was the kid. You know: 'Get the kid to do it ... He'll shovel all the black sand and do all the other things we don't want to do.' When they tipped the molten steel, I had to stand in front of it with a big, long steel rake, pushing the slag back. It was hot-as-buggery, singe-your-eyebrows-off sort of stuff.

stubbies

Originally the brand name of a style of very short shorts. When I worked on the Sydney Harbour Bridge, the builders' uniform was footy socks, stubbies and a black or blue singlet. That's how I fronted up when I appeared on *New Faces* as a dare from my workmates (though I went a bit upmarket and wore a shirt with the sleeves pulled off instead of a singlet). I didn't know I'd be dressing that way in public for the next ten years. Fortunately, we have a warm sunny, country. Just the thing for stubbies, though I have to agree they haven't aged well. A year or two ago, the divine Olivia Newton-John was on *The View* with Whoopi Goldberg, and they had four or five ladies looking at, and laughing at, a photo of Liv and me meeting the Queen after our Opera House performance in 1980. The Queen's in her regal clobber, with a full crown; Liv's in a beautiful, long, red evening gown; and I'm next to her in my stubbies, sleeveless shirt and footy socks. So it looks like the Queen's a regal Corgi, Liv's best in show, like a beautiful golden retriever, while I'm a blue heeler with an ear missing that's somehow been dragged into the middle. The women on *The View* all had a giggle and said, 'Why's he wearing hot pants in front of the Queen?' They weren't hot pants. They were stubbies, and millions of Australians wore them back then. In America shorts weren't short. They went down to your knees. They still do. They play in basketball shorts that aren't short at all. No place for Warwick Capper there.

In my second year I thought, *Yeah, it's great for Johnny, he's gonna own it. But I'm not. I'm gonna be here in this horrible heat, being everybody's labourer.* The penny had finally dropped. *Here I am in the land of opportunity and I'm shovelling black sand all day. This is a shit job! There's got to be more to life than working in an iron foundry.*

So I worked on the roads, the railways and in construction, but I'd usually leave those jobs each summer to work as a pool attendant at Granville pool. I was at 'the baths' over quite a few Christmases. It was such a great job. I'd been kicked out of there when I was fourteen for horsing around on the diving towers, and now it was my job to kick out the troublemakers.

Best of all, that job gave me my own private Olympic-size swimming pool at night. In the summer it would stay open till nine o'clock or thereabouts. I'd lock up, turn off the lights and take the key, and go to the pub or the milk bar. At the end of the night, I'd yell out, 'Who wants to go for a swim?' Great for picking up birds too.

It's hard to imagine now how big a deal that was: to have a 'private' swimming pool in the Western Suburbs of Sydney, where nobody had a private pool. We'd never even heard of such a thing.

Invasion of the teenager

In the mid-fifties there weren't even jeans in Australia. Imagine a world without jeans, and with every male wearing a short-back-and-sides haircut.

Suddenly, we saw Marlon Brando on the screen in *The Wild One*, and we saw Elvis Presley, the King, and James Dean, my personal hero, in *Rebel Without a Cause* and *East of Eden*. And we heard the word *teenager* and, for the first time, it was cool to be in that awkward stage between wearing short pants and being an adult with a job and a family and all that. Teenage culture came out of nowhere and seemed to dominate everything. We had rock 'n' roll and then television with all these American shows, and you'd start to see square cuts and buzz cuts and people trying to look like Elvis, with quiffs.

We had our own rock 'n' rollers too. Johnny O'Keefe was our first homegrown hero. If you heard any Australian music before J.O.K. rocked our world, it was Smoky Dawson or Slim Dusty or some other Australian country music singer. Johnny O'Keefe couldn't sing very well, and had no sense of rhythm, but it didn't matter. He used to belt it out and we loved him.

All this activity made our politicians look even older, and more out of touch. Prime Minister Robert Menzies seemed like something from the 1920s.

Bodgies and widgies

The rise of J.O.K. was accompanied by the rise of bodgies and widgies. Bodgies were the boys and widgies the girls who took on a 'rocker' lifestyle. There was fear in the newspapers and talk of dangerous gangs and things. But, frankly, being a bodgie or widgie usually meant not much more than wearing a square cut, or a flat top, or a bad imitation of Elvis's hairdo, and perhaps a leather jacket in honour of Marlon Brando or James Dean.

The press complained that, with the longer hair of the boys and the girls cutting their hair short and wearing jeans

Our king of rock 'n' roll, Johnny O'Keefe, is here being interviewed by Radio 4TO announcer Stewart 'Stuie' McInnes in 1969. J.O.K. could belt it out like no one else.

(often so they could climb onto the back of a motorcycle), it was getting hard to tell boys from girls. They obviously didn't know what was coming!

We were in our mid-teens when the trend hit Granville. The biggest bodgie rebellion act was to get a rocker haircut, so my mate Paul brought scissors and a razor to school and I became his booking agent. I'd sidle up to people and whisper, 'Want to get a square cut?', then I'd collect the money and set up the appointments, one after another at lunchtime or straight after school. Paul'd give them a new haircut and I'd handle the money. The parents and teachers were scandalised.

Kids had mop-tops in the early 1960s, thanks to the Beatles, and then the really long rock-star hair arrived in the 1970s. In each case it caused outrage. But you can't really shock anyone with a haircut anymore, can you? Look at sport! Cricketers and footballers have always had some pretty weird haircuts, but during Covid they became even more extreme. You looked at almost any haircut in sport and thought, *If he didn't do that himself, or get his wife to do it, his hairdresser should be shot.* And just when you thought a haircut couldn't be worse than this guy's, you'd see the next guy, and realise you were wrong.

The one that freaks me out is the Kim Jong-un coiffure, with the shaving around the side, the brush-back on top and the rises on each side like horns. Kim's the one guy who thought, wrongly, that he could get away with it, even though it's just real dopey and makes your ears stick out. And then I noticed some young Australians and Americans were into it. I thought, *Why? That's Kim Jong-un's haircut!* You're not even allowed to get one of them in North Korea, unless you're him.

Making it big

Marlon Brando famously said in the film *On the Waterfront* that he coulda been a contender. I could have been one too. Many of the blokes I went to school with, and worked with, thought the same way. We dreamt of making it big in some way or another. But it wasn't to get a ticket out of the Western Suburbs, as some might have thought. It never even occurred to most of us to get out of the place. We were happy there.

My first attempt to make it big was in diving. Then it was boxing. At one stage I even thought there might be a cushy living to be earnt as a professional punter. The thing I ended up doing was the thing I least expected.

When I had a cerebral haemorrhage in 1986, the press pushed their way into the hospital with me. As long as I was thought to be in my last days, the coverage was wonderful. They quoted people who knew me saying what an amazing person I was, a virtual saint, and all the papers noted that I'd been a

THE SIX O'CLOCK
SWILL

During World War I, a law came in that said pubs had to shut at 6 p.m. This law was partly influenced by war shortages, but also probably designed to ensure working blokes who weren't overseas serving their country turned up at the factories and building sites the next day, rather than staying out on the turps. When the war finished, six o'clock closing continued, and it meant that once the publican said, 'Last call, gentlemen', an incredibly large amount of alcohol was ordered and consumed quickly. Very, very quickly. This became known as the six o'clock swill.

The six o'clock swill was still happening when I was a teenager. Me and my mates weren't allowed to go into pubs because we were too young, but we'd still go to Plasto's Hotel and sit across the road after six to watch the fights. Blokes would all be tumbling out of the hotel, shit-faced and bulletproof and there'd be blues going on everywhere. Watching drunks fight was so much fun! Truly, if someone was selling tickets, I'd have bought one. It was like World Championship Wrestling with biting and scratching thrown in, and a good deal of language that was somewhat educational for any passing migrants!

Sadly, as some would say, the six o'clock swill finished in New South Wales in 1955, when pubs were allowed to stay open until 10 p.m. Good thing television was just around the corner or we would have been starved of entertainment.

A place apart

When I was an apprentice moulder at the iron foundry in the suburb of Clyde, the Locomotive Hotel was across the road. There was a bloke who would pull up in the car park each afternoon with his missus and run into the pub, leaving her in the car. The next minute he'd rush out again, carrying a small glass of beer, a middy, and he'd pass it to her through the window, then go back inside the pub on his own.

A lot of my workmates were saying, 'What a kind and considerate bloke, what a gentleman.' I wasn't so sure. I was only fifteen, but I thought he was being bossed around by his wife. I might not see it that way today.

Of course, this bloke would never take her inside because the main bar was only for men. You wouldn't see women in there, except for the barmaid. If the husband and wife wanted to sit together – and it looked like in this case neither of them did – they'd have to stay in the Ladies' Lounge.

The idea of the Ladies' Lounge was to create a less rowdy part of the pub so a woman could have a drink without being subjected to a bunch of drunken men. It was also so that any man who wanted to include his spouse or would-be spouse in his social circle could bring her to the pub and maybe meet up with, say, Fred and his wife. But men could not go into the Ladies' Lounge on their own.

The Ladies' Lounge also had the six o'clock swill, so perhaps they hit the sherry real hard at the end, I don't know. From what I glimpsed through the window, it was all old ladies hunched over tiny drinks, with just the occasional brave bloke escorting one of them.

potential Olympic diver. But no, I hadn't. I'd only been runner-up in the state championships. It was my friend Mickey Baker who'd had a far better chance of representing our country, at the 1956 Olympics. Every dive he did was graceful, and he hit the water each time with scarcely a splash. I felt like a bag of potatoes next to him. But he died at seventeen. Not from a diving accident but from Hodgkin's lymphoma. So sad. I was never going to be as good as Mickey.

We divers were few and far between, because only two pools in Sydney had regulation diving towers back in the 1950s: the North Sydney pool next to Luna Park, and Granville. And it was Granville that dominated. The Australian Junior Diving Troop was featured in the *Australian Women's Weekly*, and we were almost all Granville boys. The pride of the suburb!

Our trainer, Wally Lucas, was an old fat guy whose signature dive was to go out to the end of the board and flop onto his arse then bounce up onto his feet and then do his dive. It was his job to work us up from the one-metre board to the three-metre board, and then on to the ten-metre board. You had to do it on guts, and a bit of planning in advance. Which is to say you'd always wear a pullover or a footy jumper when you were learning, to take some of the sting out of landing flat on your back, which we did quite a bit. We used to be warned about the speed we'd be travelling at if we were also rotating to do a two-and-a-half and ended up going flat. They told us we'd be hitting the water at forty-two miles an hour or something like that. That's nearly seventy clicks, and water feels like concrete at that speed.

night on the tiles

A *night on the tiles* means a night at the pub. (It's not to be confused with a *night on the turps*, though a night on the turps could lead to a night on the tiles if you find yourself lying on the bathroom floor after driving the porcelain bus.) The original expression came about because all pubs once had tiled floors and walls. That was so that after all the fighting, beer slopping and chundering of the six o'clock swill, the premises could be hosed down. *On the tiles* simply meant you were at the pub.

Fast hands

There was no Granville football team of any code. We had the swimming pool and the boxing gymnasiums and that was it. So when I decided I'd gone as far as I was going to go in diving, I switched to boxing. The problem with diving is that being fearless isn't enough. You're either naturally graceful, like Mickey, or you're not. You can practise more, but you can't try harder. When you're boxing, however, even if you start badly, you can improve mid-bout and eventually win. Okay, not if you're knocked out in the first ten seconds, but hopefully that wasn't going to happen.

My boxing apprenticeship was long. I was still trying to make something of myself as a boxer when I started on the Bridge, still dreaming of being welterweight champion of the world. But there comes a time when reality sets in. I'd started well, winning a string of fights, but always on points. There used to be two great trainers of pro boxers in Sydney, Bill McConnell and Ern McQuillan, and McConnell said to me, 'You know son, you've got lovely fast hands. But you get ahead of people, and you coast instead of finishing them off. There's no mongrel in you.' It was true enough. I did have fast hands. But once I could see in the other boxer's eyes that he wasn't going to get anywhere, I would just sort of back off and win it on points.

I met boxer Joe Bugner – 'Aussie Joe Bugner' – much later. He had come up with a half-baked script in which I was going to play his older brother. He was the gentle giant, and I was the little mean guy. People would try to pick fights with him in the pub and I'd come up and knock them out. The film was never made, but I really enjoyed Big Joe's company.

Joe kept fighting until he was about fifty. He was, as they say, built like a Greek statue, and he had the same number of moves. Joe'd just stand there, trading blows. He used to say when you're fighting someone, you want to end it quickly, before they get too hurt. So knocking your opponent unconscious is not cruel; you are doing them a favour. I never saw it that way, alas. I lacked the killer instinct.

In my day, boxing was a mainstream sport, much more than any type of fighting is today. How big boxing was in each part of Sydney depended on how many gyms there were in that area. Granville had plenty. Maybe that was why there was a lot of street fighting too.

biff artist

Someone keen to go the fist, for whom a good night out involves a blue or a barney with some other punters.

Saturday night's not all right

There are certain traditions you grow up with and just accept. And then when you look back you think, *What the hell was that about?* One of them for me was the tradition that Friday night was fight night and Saturday night was date night. And so it was that Friday nights consisted of going to the pub with your mates and then, when it got to about eight or nine o'clock and you'd be pissed, you'd all leave, looking for trouble. It was never hard to find. Outside the pub, or on the walk back home, someone would niggle you, or you'd niggle them (I was a mouthy bugger, I'll admit), and next thing you were having a stoush.

A guy named Garry was one of the Granville boys we'd drink with. He was a bit of a boofhead and he was really getting on my nerves one Friday night. We were walking back in the same direction and I said something to him, and then he said something to me, and our voices were getting louder and I threw a punch, or he did. Either way, it was on. I was winning too, but suddenly our mini, moving brawl stumbled into a well-lit place, which was a row of shops with a cop car sitting right outside. So we both dropped our mitts, and I put my arm around Garry's shoulder and we walked away like the best of mates.

Fights like that proved you didn't even need to go outside your own group to find trouble. But we did anyway. We had lots of fights with the Auburn Boys, from the next suburb. It was a bit like *West Side Story*, but with a lot less singing and dancing.

Now we have kick boxing, MMA, cage fighting and more, ideas about fairness in fighting have changed. We used to look down on anyone who used their boots in a fight. We called them *slipper merchants*. It was really frowned upon, a sort of low-class thuggery. 'Better belt him quick because he's a slipper merchant. If he gets you down, he'll put the boot into you.' Yes, there was a code of honour even in street fighting.

Right place, wrong time

Saturday was date night, and you'd often have a black eye or bruised hands, depending how you'd gone the night before. On date night, you'd take your girlfriend to the pictures. That's all dates ever were. You'd never go to a restaurant – that was way too flash. We'd eat at our separate houses – at six o'clock – and then meet up.

I remember an exception: I went to a coffee bar in Granville with Noelene (who I ended up marrying). Coffee bars didn't much exist in the Australian suburbs in the 1950s, so this was new and exciting. It had been set up by some Lebanese people, and recent Lebanese immigrants were the main customers.

This was a racist time, alas, and a couple of my mates arrived that night and quietly asked me, 'What are you doing in here?'

'Er, having a coffee.'

'Well, hurry up, we need you to grab your date and leave because we're about to thump these wogs.'

bludging

Taking it easy. Also known as shirking, but it's not always a negative. As long as you pull your weight when needed, everyone is entitled to 'have a bit of a bludge' every now and then. Someone who has no interest in finding work can be derogatively called a *dole bludger*. But some people who have found work are bludgers too. An example: when I was laying train tracks between Lidcombe and Granville in the 1950s, the ganger – or boss – was a gnarly old bloke named Ned. He was raised in the Great Depression, which was so tough it defined people for the rest of their lives. He'd laid railway tracks himself back then, back when his ganger would walk along the line and, if he wasn't happy with someone, he'd just throw them a shilling. That was it, they were off, and unemployed, and very likely soon starving. With that sort of background, you can imagine how lovable Ned was. He constantly walked up and down to inspect our work, looking grumpy and ready to pounce. But as soon as he walked past, everyone stopped. I was a bit shocked by this at first, but I soon got into the groove. We'd be knuckling down, hammering spikes and carting rails, but the minute Ned passed, everyone had a bludge. And it stayed that way until he reached the end of his walk and turned around. Then we'd all work again. I don't know if he knew what was happening, but as long as he wasn't looking, nobody did a thing. It wasn't the most efficient work gang, I'll admit. Bunch of bludgers really.

My mates were looking after me, as they saw it. They didn't want me to be in the middle of a blue while I was with my girlfriend. Why was there going to be a blue? Because my mates resented the fact that the coffee shop was full of wogs. Didn't matter that these mates of mine included a Greek, an Italian, a Welshman and, bizarrely, Eddie, who was second-generation Lebanese himself. They saw the new arrivals as interlopers.

Yep, there's a lot that's improved in Australia!

The bludge

There was conscription during World War II, and between 1951 and 1959 they started it again. All men in Australia turning eighteen were called up for training in the army, navy or air force. I was one of the 227,000 young blokes required to do 176 days of military service, in my case in the army.

I quite enjoyed my short time in uniform, but, unfortunately, being drafted cost me a really cruisy, well-paying job. I was working the night shift at the Shell Oil refinery at Clyde. I'd further adjusted my birth certificate when I started that job (after putting it up a year to get my motorcycle licence) and was pulling an adult wage as a supposed twenty-one-year-old. Companies were obliged to keep a job open for anyone who was doing their national service, but if I'd said anything I would have been busted, as twenty-one-year-olds didn't get drafted. So I decided I'd better quickly resign.

It was a strange job, that one. When I applied, they never asked about my education, training or anything. They just asked if I was a good diver. You see, Larry Peters, a diving mate from the Granville pool, already had a job there and had recommended me because Shell wanted to boost its sports teams.

They had these annual sports competitions against other oil companies: a big pool meet with swimming and diving, and a track and field day, and winning was very important to them. I was a decent enough short-distance swimmer and quick on my feet too, although again only over short distances.

How to Speak 'STRAYAN

flat out like a lizard drinking

Means you are hard at it, really getting into your work. No time to spare. It doesn't mean having a sleep, even though that's what lizards spend much of their days doing.

And that was my only qualification: I knew nothing about oil, or the oil industry, or chemistry (I was a lab assistant), but I was treasured because I could swim, dive and run. Another example of the power of sport in Australia.

For my job I'd walk around the huge plant collecting samples. I'd do one or two minor tests too, but most were done by the chemists. The thing I did most was sleep. As long as I went out at least twice to pick up samples, the rest of the time I could curl up in my lab and snore away. What a great bludge! I was awake all day and sleeping at night and getting paid for it.

The part I feel a little guilty about is that I beat Larry, who'd got me the job, and so it was me and not him who represented Shell at the first diving meet. I made it to the final but came in second to the Australian champion, Merv Betts. Merv had a job with a different oil company on the same basis as me, as did various mates who were good at running, jumping, swimming or diving. I always wondered who did the actual work at those places.

How to Speak 'STRAYAN

up the duff

Pregnant! There's a few variants: *bun in the oven* and all that. In the 1950s and 1960s people would say, 'She's joined the pudding club.' The ladies did not like that expression. Particularly those who were in the pudding club.

Married ~~with~~ as children

I got hitched at nineteen. It wasn't a great passionate thing, because we were just kids. About two-thirds of my mates were all married before they were twenty. That was the way it was.

At nineteen, I was a galoot. But if you got into your twenties and you weren't wed, people worried about you. So we all got married. We used to laugh at American movies when they showed the college kids, and they all looked thirty or something.

Getting my life experience early – and doing lots of hard, hot, dirty jobs – was a good thing because when I did finally land the job I loved, which was working in entertainment, I had a real appreciation of what most people have to do to earn a living. But it was a fluke. You might have the potential to be a great violinist, but if no one ever hands you a violin …

'Get married young, before they start worrying about you.' That was the unspoken message back then.

It took a succession of unlikely events for me to move from the Bridge to television, then to the big screen. Even in a land of opportunity, people who have success need to acknowledge that a measure of luck is always needed. I had plenty.

Home in time for tea

Tea isn't tea, the drink. Though it can refer to that as well. Tea is the working-class name for the evening meal. You wake up and have brekkie. Then it's dinner, usually just a sanger or a meat pie, in the middle of the day. At night, it's time for tea. I was a pretty free-range kid, but the one rule was that I had to be home at six o'clock, in time for tea. It's a habit that never left me.

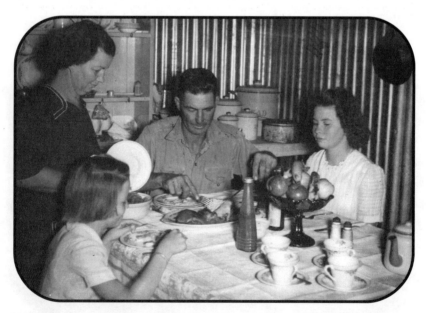

Tea: that's what everyone I knew called the evening meal. Even dads would be home for it, though it was usually pretty early. This shot shows a temporary home for workers in Townsville, Queensland. As Paul Kelly noted in his song 'How to Make Gravy', even summer's scorching heat wouldn't stop a roast.

How to Speak 'STRAYAN

chook

If it's little and fluffy, it's a chicken. If you buy it with chips from a shop, or it can lay eggs, it's a *chook*. Chick lit aimed at older readers is known in the publishing trade as *chook lit*.

snag

A *snag* is a sausage. And a good Aussie beef snag, with a little bit of tomato sauce on it, wrapped in a slice of white bread, is as good as food gets. Well, I think so.

All my friends laugh about it. My son Chance ribs me, wives have rolled their eyes: 'It's six, guess who's going to be hanging around the kitchen with his knife and fork.' But habits are hard to break and in all those years as a manual worker from age fifteen onwards, I'd start early and be ravenous by six. Bugger waiting until seven or even eight. I'd worked hard and I'd earnt it.

The pies have it

The Yanks had the hot dog and hamburger. We had pies. Pub food is now fancy but, back in the day, the choice of cuisine at a pub ranged from a meat pie to a meat pie with peas.

If you needed something on a Friday night to help soak up the beer, you'd ask Daphne for a pie. There'd be a little grill under the counter for heating it up and then your pie would be slapped on the soggy bar in a brown paper bag. At a fancier pub, it would be heated in a kitchen and served on a plate ... with mashed peas on top. They were always the pale green peas that come in a can; you never saw the bright green fresh ones on your pie. And you never wished for those either. Nah, the pale green ones were just right.

Most of the time, a pie was eaten only with sauce. It was considered the great Aussie dish. One of the characters I did on television, Arthur Dunger, was modelled on a pot-bellied cricket fan. He used to say, 'It's only a good pie if it dribbles

Dinki Di Dogs Eyes Pies from the Kakkadoo Kafe in Dunedoo, NSW. That's peak Australia, surely. The menu notes: 'We offer a wide range of takeaway food, salads and prepared meals along with our ever popular Dinky Di Dogs Eyes home-made pies.'

sanga, sanger

A sandwich. We add an *a* sound to the end. Why there's a *g* in there, I don't know. But there is, and if you said 'sander' instead, you'd be talking something other than proper Australian, and no one would have a clue what you were on about. You certainly wouldn't get fed.

all down the front of me shirt and me wife says, "You're a disgusting pig." When she says that, I know I've had a good pie.' And that's true. The gravy has to run out of them. The pie should be burning hot, and the beer near freezing cold.

A meat pie is a brilliant piece of design because you can hold it in one hand and a beer in the other. I fear though that it's disappeared a bit as the national eating-out meal. And so-called gourmet pies are making the problem worse. It's becoming harder to get a pie with just beef in it. They have shallots and mushrooms and herbs and all sorts of completely unnecessary things in them. No, just give me beef.

AUSSIE GOURMET DELIGHTS

The Chiko Roll

In later years, you could get a Chiko Roll as pub food. Talk about sophistication. The Chiko Roll is a uniquely Australian item, inspired by the Chinese spring roll. It was originally the Chicken Roll, but people pointed out there was not a skerrick of meat in it – no chicken, or any other any meat. It was mainly oily fried cabbage and other stuff you didn't want to know about. So a name change was arranged.

The Chiko Roll is an icon and to celebrate its fiftieth anniversary the current manufacturer created gold-plated Chiko Roll replicas. Here's one of them in the Museum of the Riverina in Wagga Wagga, NSW.

You mostly bought a Chiko Roll at a fish and chip shop, but pubs served them too, and they were a big success. Then, suddenly, we started to see people eating hamburgers in American films, and we all wanted those instead.

The Greek burger

Hamburgers were never served in pubs. Too complicated. And there were no hamburger chains. You had to go to a Greek milk bar. And, funnily enough, because hamburgers were first sold here in Greek milk bars, we actually thought that they were a Greek dish. In our defence, there wasn't a lot of foreign food around at the time.

In American films (and, later, television shows), teenagers hung around something very similar to one of our Greek milk bars, though they called it a *drugstore*. We thought that was a weird name.

For us, Peter's Milk Bar at Granville, run by two Greek guys both named Peter, was the place to be. Until we were old enough to get into the pub, we'd all meet there and hang out and chase girls. Peter's was quite flash too, with chrome and glass, and Laminex-covered tables and plastic chairs, which were considered really modern. You'd eat hamburgers, because the Peters really knew how to make great burgers, but you'd never eat any real Greek food, because they never served it. I had Greek mates, but they too ate hamburgers. On the drink front, coffee wasn't a thing. We'd have Coca-Cola, strawberry malted milkshakes or maybe tea.

Most importantly, Peter's had a jukebox, where we could hear the new rock 'n' roll music from America. So the Americanisation of Australia happened with help from the Greeks.

Meat, three veg – and spag bol

At home, a typical meal was meat and three vegetables, every night. And when I say meat, we ate fried brains, a lot, and pig trotters – my mum loved those too! You only had chicken at Christmas and the like. It was a luxury. Yet lamb chops, now so much more expensive than chicken, used to be as cheap as it came. Then the Italians arrived with spaghetti and all sorts of wonderful things. These 'exotic' foods crept into the house eventually, but first they were a restaurant thing, as the Italians and Greeks were very quick to open up eateries.

Beer or sherry?

Dad would have a beer occasionally at home, but always before dinner, not with it. And Mum might have a slight sherry with him. But no one we knew drank wine. That was something we were still to learn from the Italians.

The pav

When it came to desserts, the pavlova ruled, and it still does. Once, in the 1980s, when we'd finished our mains in a restaurant in Western Australia, our waiter offered us the 'pav-a-lo-va' and told us it was named after a famous Russian dancing sheila who'd come down to Australia. I hadn't been expecting the history lesson, but I found out he was right. The Russian ballerina Anna Pavlova toured Australia in the 1920s and it's likely that Bert Sachse, the chef at the Esplanade Hotel in Perth, later created the dish in her honour. The New Zealanders claim it was their invention. They can't have it. Too tasty.

The lamington

Don't think the Kiwis have ever placed a claim on the lamington, but if they do, they can't have that one either. I love a lamington. My mum used to make them (she did a good pav as well). The best ones have a layer of jam in the middle, which sets off the chocolate and coconut perfectly. We have Lady Lamington to thank for this Australian delicacy, or her chef perhaps. She was the wife of the Governor of Queensland, Lord Lamington (1896–1901) and the first to serve them. She was clearly a lady of good taste.

CHAPTER 6

Surf, Snow, Beer and Skittles

Our idea of fun

As little kids, my mates and I would drop paddle-pop sticks into the creek and bet on which one would reach the bridge first. We'd punt on marbles at primary school, then graduate to horses and pretty well anything else from high school on. Australia's national devotion to betting is at a crazy level, but there are plenty of other things we go mad for. We are fervent beachgoers, lifesavers, surfers, motorcycle riders, movie watchers (and makers) and even skiers. And we don't mind a drink in between.

Our lives in their hands

I am constantly amazed by Aussie beaches. You can be on a perfect stretch of sand and be the only person in miles.

Bondi were the Surf Life Saving Australia Premiers, circa 1935. Here they are doing their march-past.

And ever since we learnt the joys of ocean swimming and bodysurfing, we've become a beach nation. But if you want to throw on your togs and take a dip in the waves, you'll need someone standing by, ready to save you if things go south. This is where lifesavers come in.

Lifesaving originated in Australia, way back in 1907, as a response to some drownings at Sydney beaches. It was part of a tradition of volunteering, and surf lifesaving and volunteering are as strong as ever today. The movement is still saving lives all around the country, and training 'Nippers', young kids who learn to be fit and safe in the water and will make up the next generation of surf-lifesaving volunteers.

I can tell you a bit about it through my own experience. Unlikely as it seems, my introduction came through motorcycles. Our group all had motorbikes at sixteen or seventeen. Huey, an older guy we knew, also got around on two wheels, but he was a fair bit smarter than us: he always wore a suit while on his motorcycle. That meant he never, ever got pulled over by the police, even though he tore around the place like a madman. The rest of us were all dressed as Marlon Brando in *The Wild One*, which was like an invitation to the boys in blue.

Huey was trying to recruit young guys for lifesaver training because he and his brother Brycey had a house on Era Beach in the Royal National Park south of Sydney, and they were having trouble getting lifesavers down there. We were interested because it sounded like fun, and I was particularly interested because Huey had a younger sister, and I had a crush on her. Jan was her name and she was a bit of a babe. Soon six of us, all Westies with motorbikes, were riding out to Coogee Beach in Sydney's Eastern Suburbs to get our bronze medallions for resuscitation and the like, so we'd qualify as surf lifesavers.

Era Beach was sixty kilometres or so from Granville. It had a little dirt road down to it, and the whole valley was studded with shacks and weekenders. One of the benefits was that not only did we get to go to a wild and beautiful beach, but also there was a clubhouse where we could stay overnight. For us Westies, it was a free weekend by the surf.

I'd just turned sixteen but had doctored a birth certificate to say I was a year older, because you couldn't get your learner's permit until you were sixteen and nine months, or your provisional licence, or Ps, until you were seventeen. My mates were all a bit older, so I had to play the system a bit, because having your licence was everything.

I'd like to say our surf-lifesaving impulses were down to our nobility and our urge to help our fellow man, but the chance to get chicks was a part of it too. That's basically what lifesavers do – they can get birds all the time, right? We joined the Era Beach surf lifesavers on that pretext. There were six in a team and there were six of us, and that suited us fine.

Reel life

In the 1950s, surf lifesavers still used the old reel and rope system. A harness was attached to the end of a rope on a reel, and one lifesaver, called the belt man in our day, would attach the harness to his mid-section and swim out to the person in trouble while the other team members paid out the rope above their heads. The belt man would reach the struggling swimmer, and hold their head above water as the two were pulled back in. Of course the belt man was the hero of the operation because he performed the actual rescue.

The old reel and rope system, this one on St Kilda beach in Melbourne. How this lifesaver expected to be able to do the job without the proper cap, I've got no idea.

On the very first day we had our very first incident. A guy out the back got dumped a couple of times, and his hand went up. Me and my mate Black Les – he was a Thursday Islander and that's what he called himself – were just wandering along the beach at the time. When we realised what was happening, we raced over to get into the belt and make our first rescue.

With him and me trying to get into the one belt at the same time, there was pushing and shoving and we ended up rolling around in the sand, battling each other to be the hero. We completely missed the fact that while we were going at it hammer and tongs, a couple of the other guys had just calmly dived in and swum out. By the time we picked ourselves up and spat out the sand, they'd already finished the rescue. Bugger!

Wart to the rescue

Having that unpaid rescue service was an Australian thing – still is. You were not only unpaid, you had to pay your dues to the association. Yet it never had problems getting volunteers. Now there are some lifeguards who get paid, but the backbone of the service is still, and has always been, the volunteer surf lifesavers.

Les and I did eventually make a few rescues in the belt. But most of the time we'd just dive in and swim out without the rope. It was all great fun, except for one day when a couple of fishermen were washed off the rocks. There was a really big sea and the beach was closed. We weren't even on patrol that day, just living the life on the beach, probably getting into the beer in the clubhouse. We saw it happening and ran down to the water's edge, thinking, *What are we going to do?* We were only sixteen and the waves were terrifying and the fishermen were in all sorts of trouble, and we were nervously contemplating jumping in.

How to Speak 'STRAYAN

budgie smugglers

We've always had bathers and cossies and swimming togs. But what we used to call speedos suddenly became *budgie smugglers*. Once you've realised where that name comes from, you'll never get the image out of your head – and you'll feel very sorry for budgies. On my first trip to America in the early 1970s I met up with a friend of mine, Bob Rich. He was an American who did some work for *A Current Affair* in Australia. I'd just arrived at a big hotel and suggested Bob meet me down at the pool. So I turned up in my budgie smugglers and suddenly everything went quiet and everyone was looking at me. Bob was horrified. 'Jeez, don't wear those out here,' he whispered. 'The only people who wear those are European gays.' He was right; every bloke, including Bob, was in baggy swim shorts. But swimming in baggy shorts is stupid. You never see anyone in the Olympics wearing baggy shorts. And divers always wear speedos. They just make sense. No matter what you call them.

Wart swam straight out and saved the guy who still had his head above the water, then went out again ...

Fortunately, there was an older guy named Wart on the beach. That was his nickname, and Wart was beefy and covered in black hair. Hard as nails. Chunky guy, really strong swimmer. He grabbed us and told us to stay put, which was a relief at the time; I'm sure we wouldn't have been able to handle it. We could still see one guy, but the other one had gone under. Wart swam straight out and saved the guy who still had his head above the water, then went out again and brought in the body of the other.

That was distressing. It was the first dead body I'd seen, and although one bloke had been saved, Les and I felt ashamed. We thought we should have dived in straight away, and then maybe the three of us could have saved them both. I remember it so well because it was my first brush with death.

How to Speak 'STRAYAN

Noah

A surfer's term for a shark, as in, 'We saw a big Noah out the back today.' Rhyming slang, from Noah's ark.

shark biscuit

A boogie board, sometimes with a kid on it, out there in the surf, like a snack floating around.

Surf's up

It was seven years after the founding of surf lifesaving in Australia when Duke Paoa Kahinu Mokoe Hulikohola Kahanamoku visited the country. Simply known as The Duke, for pretty obvious reasons, he introduced Australians to surfboard riding by giving a demonstration at Freshwater Beach in Sydney in late 1914. He was a Hawaiian, and surfing was a Hawaiian invention, but The Duke counts as an honorary Aussie. After all, he taught us one of the best things we could do with our beaches, and we have the most beaches in the world – ten thousand of them.

This shot of Duke Kahanamoku (and friend) was taken in California, but he had a huge impact here. The Duke taught us how to surf.

My favourite surfing moment was in that competition in South Africa in 2015 when Australian champion Mick Fanning had this huge fin come up next to him. When the shark knocked him off his board, Fanning started punching it in the back. And his mate, fellow Australian Julian Wilson, paddled over to give him a hand. Anyone else from anywhere else in the world would have raced off the other way.

We have a reputation for this kind of thing. I was on Fairfield Beach in Connecticut in the US with my daughter and grandchildren. They had these marker buoys, and you weren't supposed to go beyond them. We were standing near the lifeguard tower, and there was a lively discussion going on between the lifeguards because some people were swimming past the buoys. One said: 'We need to call them back in.' The other guy said: 'It's all right, they're Australians.'

Now, you might think he meant they're Australians, so we can afford to lose them, but I'm sure he meant, 'No, they'll be right, they're used to swimming with sharks down there. If they see any, they'll probably just go all Mick Fanning on 'em.' Other countries jump the shark. We give it a knuckle sandwich.

Not waving, drowning

One weekend there was a surf lifesaving carnival at Era, with teams from nearby Garie Beach and Wattamolla Beach. In our Era club, I was usually the fastest swimmer and Black Les was the strongest. He boasted that he could swim all day, and he really could. We ended up in different Era teams in the same belt race at the carnival, which involved attaching yourself to the lifesaving reel harness and swimming out to a buoy.

Era Beach, with a crowd surrounding a surf boat. I may even be in the shot somewhere. It was wild and basic and out of the way, but Era was a getaway paradise for us Westies.

When you reached the buoy, you put your arm up and your crew pulled you towards the sand as quickly as possible. The first to get their swimmer back on shore was the winning crew.

There was a fairly heavy sea, with tons of seaweed. I was expected to reach the buoy first, so my crew was looking out there, on the ready. After a bit, they saw an arm go up over the choppy sea and assumed it was me. But it wasn't. It was Les, whose strength had enabled him to do a much better job of ploughing through the seaweed.

The crew started pulling me in towards the beach while I was still swimming away from it. As they were trying to haul me in, I was being dragged back, and dragged under. And I had almost a ton of seaweed on me, which was pulling me down further. For safety's sake, you had a pin in the front of your belt, which you could pull out if something like this happened. But being sixteen, I hadn't bothered checking it when I picked up my gear, like you were supposed to. The pin was bent and I couldn't get it out.

Soon I was down about fifteen feet or more below the surface, trying to get the pin out, and eventually giving up. I'd heard from other people that a strange calmness comes over you when you are going to drown. And it did. I remember thinking, *Oh well, I can't get the pin out, that's me done,* and then I stopped struggling. What I should have done, I realised later, was to grab the rope behind me and pull myself along until I could slip the belt off over my noggin. But no, I just decided I was going to drown.

I have to admit my youthful fascination with lifesaving had a lot to with increasing my chances of meeting girls. The cap showed everyone you were a man of action and public service. It didn't quite work for Strop, though.

Fortunately, Freddie Holloway, the club captain, was out in the boat near the buoys. He realised what was happening and came over. Two of the guys dived off the boat and came down and brought me to the surface. I emerged, spluttering and moaning.

Freddie and his crew had saved my life. But when you're sixteen, it's no big deal. There was no expression of eternal gratitude. I just said, 'Oh, good on you guys.'

About ten years ago I did my back in. I couldn't move and was in so much pain I had to go to hospital. Somehow Freddie found out. He sent a message to my hospital room saying it was good to make contact after all these years and, by the way, I hadn't paid my dues for the past fifty years. A bill was enclosed. I had to laugh, which hurts when your back's playing up. Freddie's letter also reminded me you don't do lifesaving for the money.

You're swimming in it

In 1971 I was given a bravery award for stopping someone jumping off the Bridge. I was embarrassed to get it because the other people queuing up with me to receive their medals had had to overcome their fears to get their awards, whereas I hadn't been scared at all. Heights never fazed me. I was as comfortable up there as I was with my two feet on solid ground. The award should have been for being fearless and stupid.

Generally, I've never been someone to get scared. I didn't feel any fear when I nearly drowned as a teenager. But when my daughter, Loren, was two years old, she went missing on the beach. I was talking to someone and turned my back and she'd gone. And that was the first time in my life that I experienced that instant terror that other people talk about.

The public pool was a big part of growing up for so many Aussies. Most of us learnt to swim young, but the water still brought surprises and occasional frights.

It was much more frightening than any mishap on a motorbike. My heart stopped and I went into a total panic. I'll never forget it. I grabbed a lifesaver and said 'Er ... little girl ... green costume ... ahh!'

There's a famous painting of a child all on its own in the Australian bush (*Lost* by Frederick McCubbin). That was the early fear of settlers. They didn't swim much and they certainly didn't go to beaches back in the nineteenth century. They feared the bush, as we fear drowning.

I made sure all my kids could swim by the time they were three. But you still run into adults who can't swim. I taught a couple of guys who worked on the Bridge with me to swim, two Scotsmen. Trust me, the hardest people to teach to swim are adults. They don't like having their face put underwater. So, two grown Scotsmen, a hell of a job.

SNOW TIME

It's easy to understand why we dominated world swimming for so long. We had the best beaches, and more of them than anyone else. And, for a long time, there was no TV. So there was nothing else to do. But it is even more amazing that although about 99 percent of our population have never skied or skated, we still compete at Olympic level at winter sports, against countries that are under snow for about ten months of the year.

We started pretty early, back in 1861, when three Norwegians formed the Kiandra Snow Shoe Club. But they didn't do it in Norway, they did it in the town of Kiandra, New South Wales.

They made skis – which were then called snowshoes – and formed what is now recognised as the oldest ski club in the world. In Australia, for goodness sake, a country where 1 percent of this whole continent gets enough snow to even scoop up!

I never skied in Australia. Never knew anyone who did, unless they lived in Victoria somewhere near the mountains. Not much snow in Granville. Not much at Kosciuszko either for that matter. (Mt Kosciuszko is our tallest hill at a slightly pathetic 2228 metres; that's about three thousand metres lower than Everest's Base Camp.)

When I started skiing at nearly sixty, I hadn't even walked on snow until that point. It was at Aspen in the US, and when they turned up with an instructor for me, it was a woman. I was a bit old-school and said, 'I can't have a woman teaching me.' They said, 'She's an Aussie, you'll be all right.' She was a Taswegian girl, fearless, a really good skier as well. Every time I skied in the States after that I'd hear the Aussie accent everywhere. It was mainly young guys and girls, going up there and working on the lifts and everything else so they could ski in their own time.

punters

Regular, ordinary sort of people. The type you like to knock about with. Or a potential paying audience ('a bunch of punters') or clients. A *punter* is also a gambler, so again this term is in line with our habit of tying everything to sport and betting. A *mug punter* is a gambler who almost always loses.

It's a punter's life

Australia is a nation of mug punters, which is to say our people are addicted to gambling and will bet on just about anything – horses, dogs, footy, cricket, car racing or even the proverbial two flies crawling up a wall.

Bookies were just everywhere. They had to be, because people wanting to have a punt were everywhere.

When I was young, betting on horse races was only permitted at the racetrack (and, from the early 1960s, through the government 'totaliser' shops, or TABs). But in almost every neighbourhood there was what was known as an SP bookie. These bookmakers would take bets from anyone, and would offer the odds as they finally stood as the race got underway – SP is short for 'starting price'. The TABs paid via a complex formula, which usually delivered less to winners.

Bookies could be found everywhere, even in places where they were legal. This is licensed bookmaker Mr Allan Scott plying his trade at Rosehill Racecourse.

My mother-in-law, Noelene's mum, was an SP bookie. Billy Harris, the barber at the house behind us, used to cut people's hair, but he also kept a book. John Cornell's dad used to run a gambling joint in Kalgoorlie, and that's where John was born. Bookies were just everywhere. They had to be, because people wanting to have a punt were everywhere.

My dad should have been a bookie because he was a maths whizz. Through the week, for most of his career, he worked for the military, but in a civilian role, as chief purchasing officer for the Army canteen service. Presumably that job involved some number crunching, but on weekends his maths skills made him much sought after, pencilling – working out odds and filling out betting sheets – for bookies.

You could throw numbers at Dad and he could calculate anything you needed. As kids we'd go to him and say, 'All right, this horse is 11/4, how much would I get if I put one pound five shillings on it, each way.' As you finished the sentence, he'd say, 'That's two pounds and 14 shillings for a place.' Or whatever was the right answer. I had to go and write it down and work it out, but as fast as you could say it, Dad'd answer. And he was always right. So he had almost a mathematical savant thing going, but he didn't bet himself, or use his maths to work out how he could make money. He was happy just pencilling for bookies on weekends.

Quallies on Satdy

Most people tended to bet on horses, but a couple of people in our street had greyhounds, the poor man's thoroughbreds. 'The dogs' were quite a thing in the day. When I was doing roadworks, there was an old guy on our crew we called Greyhound Jack, because he used to live for his dogs. He'd always say one of his mutts was in a 'qually on Satdy'. That meant it was in some sort of qualifying run on the weekend. He was always talking about 'quallies', but never races, so I think Greyhound Jack's dish-lickers weren't a super breed.

GONE TO
THE DOGS

When I was young I went with mates quite a few times to watch the dogs in the Western Suburbs, then didn't do it again until I went with my great mate and business partner John Cornell in London. Kerry Packer, who owned the television station we were working for at the time, wanted to come with us and John wouldn't let him unless he took his tie off. He finally agreed, but Big Kezza, media and cricket baron and billionaire, still stood out at the dogs. And of course he gambled like mad. Couldn't help himself. There was nothing he wouldn't punt on.

There was an advantage to being inside Kerry Packer's circle. When we were in Las Vegas filming *Hogan's America*, Corny and I went up to the front desk of this huge hotel-casino and said, 'We work for Kerry Packer, and he has recommended we stay here.'

Now Big Kezza was known for betting and losing millions at this joint, and probably lots of other joints around there too. So, at the mention of his name, we were given a vast, multi-room suite with the works. John was at one end and I was at the other, and it was a fair old walk just to meet up. When we checked out, we got a Motel Six–level bill, all fully subsidised by Kerry's gambling losses.

It was hard work on the roads, driving around in our truck, looking for cracks and divots. We had a diamond-tipped saw to make the grooves in the road deeper so we could fix them with the tar kettle. This involved pouring hot, stinking tar into the grooves to smooth up the road. Working with the tar kettle was the shittiest part of a pretty shit job. What made it bearable though was the people, good and bad. And Greyhound Jack was a good bloke, even if he was always talking about his greyhounds and the quallies.

He must have been sixty, if he was a day, and he was still pouring tar on the road and waiting for the day his dogs would change everything. But at least, unlike with horses, you could enjoy ownership without being rich.

Favoured by fortune

In 1962, or thereabouts, I was a mug punter. All punters are mug punters, I suppose. But for a little while, I was quite successful at it. I was in my early twenties and working Saturdays at a gym that doubled as an illegal weekend bookie joint. I was paid to sit in the boxing ring with a mate and, if the alarm sounded, jump up and start boxing. The police would see the fight and either believe (or pretend to believe) that this was why there were so many 'spectators' crammed into the gym.

If you spend hours and hours in a bookie joint you can't help but join in, especially if you get lucky early on with a couple of decent wins. That's what happened to me, and it got me into punting seriously. At one stage, I had a couple of thousand quid's worth of winnings in my stash, back when I was earning like £14 or £15 a week. On Saturdays I'd drag it out of my special hiding place in the toolshed and very

How to Speak 'STRAYAN

bolter

A *bolter* is a rank outsider that comes home first. Like many turns of phrase, it comes from horse racing. We say, 'That's correct weight' when something is right, we talk about people *having blinkers on*, or being *a stayer*. And terms like *long shot*, *taking a spell* (a break), *late mail* (the most up-to-date information), *front-runner* and *odds-on favourite* also come from the track. So does the idea of *write your own ticket* – do whatever you want.

carefully carry it with me to the gym. Two thousand quid! It was ridiculous – about the price of a brand new, pretty flash car. I'd have maybe five bob in my pocket for six days a week, and £2000 on a Saturday.

Being a true punter, I considered that money sacred. It was a wad of cash that no one else knew about, that I didn't use for anything else but punting. Only once did I break that rule, when I bought my wife a present – I think it was a dress. I wasn't even in the doghouse; I just thought I should buy Noelene something because I was doing well, and she deserved to share a bit in my good fortune. I never told her where the money came from, of course. She probably thought I nicked it.

Losing it

You were considered a top bloke if you knew your horses. I never got suckered into poker machines. A monkey could play those, so there was no satisfaction there. But knowing your horses brought respect. And serious punting soon became a scholarly business for me. I'd buy the paper, go through all the horses, study their form, find out how many races each horse I was interested in had been in, whether it liked a soft track or a hard track and all that, and I'd check out the opposition. You took pride in it, because you were doing the homework. And then, when you came up with a winner, you'd pat yourself on the back and know your research had paid off.

I did all my gambling at the gym, handing over my money and, along with the big crowd there, listening to the results of each race blaring over a radio speaker. I found I had the magic touch too, until … I lost the lot in two afternoons. Yep, everything. I backed the wrong horse, as they say.

I'd done my research on a champion sprinter named Star Kingdom and its progeny. The progeny turned out to be very fast too, though not fast enough to save my £2000. I was so confident, I put a pile on Star Kingdom's offspring one week. And then I bet even bigger the next Saturday to make up for my loss. The biggest single dud bet was on King Roto, out of Star Kingdom and Dorota. I thought that nag was going to get me out of trouble, and I went too heavy on it.

That was the end of my punting money. Fortunately I'd learnt the lesson that, if you're going to gamble, you have to know how much you can lose without being depressed for the rest of the week. That way I could enjoy being a punter, without risking dipping into the family money when my punting money ran out. They were two separate things. That was my mentality: you wouldn't use your punting money to buy breakfast, or put your breakfast money on the horses. When my £2000 disappeared, I gave the horses up.

Well, not entirely, because when I had to choose a name for a new company, set up to make the movie that became *Crocodile Dundee*, I went for Rimfire. That was the name of the legendary horse that won the Melbourne Cup in 1948, ridden by a fifteen-year-old jockey. Rimfire was an 80/1 rank outsider, but it proved to be a bolter, nailing Dark Marne right on the line in the Cup's first photo finish. I figured that maybe, just maybe, my pissant little rank-outsider company could do the same. And it did. Yeah, to everyone's surprise, my first little movie turned out to be a bolter too.

Beer crimes

For us blue-collar workers – I returned to being one straight after doing 'nasho', or national service – it was the tradition to go to the pub, or rubbidy-dub, at the end of a long hard working week. But you didn't go just to 'have a drink'. You went to *blow the froth off a few cold ones*, or perhaps *knock back a few schooners* (a glass containing around half a litre of beer). And the beer you went for back then defined who you were.

When I was working on the Bridge, after work on Fridays, and on other days if we could afford it (I usually couldn't), we went to the Harbour View Hotel, at the top end of The Rocks, the oldest part of Sydney. The pub was right under the southern approach to the Bridge. It's a flash pub now, but back then it was a pretty tough old joint and strictly for Bridge workers and wharfies. I remember being in there once and an old guy, Paddy, came in and got a beer off Daphne, the barmaid. He took a sip, then spat it out like it was poison. It was a huge spray, across the tiles, the bar, and past half a dozen patrons, who turned in panic.

WANKA
BY NAME ...

In the late 1960s, Evel Knievel became an international superstar by jumping his motorcycle over things – or, more often than not, not quite jumping his motorcycle over things and discovering all manner of ways to spectacularly smash himself up.

Suddenly, the world was filled with bad stuntmen, and Australia had its share of them. I remember being at a showground somewhere, watching a guy wearing the obligatory cape and striped jumpsuit leaping his motorcycle over a whole row of cars. He'd obviously painstakingly planned it all, making sure he could get his speed just right and clear the last vehicle. He touched down beautifully too. One thing though: he'd clearly forgotten to measure the distance from his likely landing spot to the picket fence that surrounded the arena.

I'm not sure what speed he was doing when he ploughed into the fence, but it wasn't pretty. And while there didn't seem to be much risk of fire, what I remember most was that all these guys came sprinting in with fire extinguishers and dowsed everything, as if saving him, his bike and the entire audience from an inferno.

It was just brilliantly daft, and thus one of the most popular characters on *The Paul Hogan Show* was born. He was Leo Wanker (well Wanka, but we'll come to that shortly). My inspiration wasn't any stuntman in particular, just vain people in general. I should remark though that we also had some really brave and talented stunt people; I know because I worked with quite a few of them. But there was no fun in sending up competent people. Nah, the self-important, slightly delusional drips are much more fun. And, believe me, there were plenty of Leo Wanker–types, who would be so self-important that when the stunts didn't work, which was almost always, they'd still have that strut going for them.

Inspired by true events, no matter what happened with a Leo stunt, and whether fire was involved or not, in almost every sketch with Leo I'd have one of his sidekicks rush in with a fire extinguisher to spray everyone and everything (always giving a special blast to the crotch). Some of my sketches from the 1970s and 1980s are very dated, but Leo still seems just as silly and just as ridiculous as he did then. No wonder Facebook has a Leo Wanker Appreciation Society.

So that you know, Leo's surname was meant to be spelt Wanka, which is a Polish name, but when the graphics were done on the suit and the truck, they spelt it Wanker. And I just said, 'Oh well, he's going to be called that instead.'

Wanker has a literal meaning, but when Australians call someone that, they generally mean that person is having himself on. A wanker thinks he's a big deal. He's got tickets on himself. And Leo was all that.

Funny, we sold these cut-up versions of the Hogan show in America. They ran at 11 o'clock at night on Channel 13 or something. When I was in Las Vegas, getting out of the swimming pool, a couple of guys approached me. 'Are you Paul Hogan?' one asked. 'We love your show, but we wanted to ask you something.' The other whispered: 'In Australia, does wanker mean what we think it means?'

I smiled and said, 'I'm sure it does.'

And that was the highlight of the show for them, a guy called Leo Wanker. I liked Leo and enjoyed playing him. A tribute came a bit later. A character appeared on US television called Super Dave, who everyone said was quite clearly based on my superstar of Polish origin.

Pub life. Your choice of beer (and sadly cigarettes) was all-important.

You see, old Paddy was a Tooheys drinker, and she'd given him a Reschs! All his mates glared at Daphne, like she'd served him battery acid, and she was so apologetic. People were all coming over and consoling the poor bloke. 'Are you all right, Paddy? Oh, mate, we're really sorry. Are you sure you're okay?' And: 'Daphne! What were you thinking?!'

How it went was the real connoisseurs drank Tooheys Old, some of the more senior blokes drank Reschs, and the upstarts like me drank Tooheys New. It was just so much a part of you, your brand of beer, that when you were at the rubbidy with your mates, you were absolutely locked into your Reschs or your Tooheys. And I probably shouldn't admit this, but I couldn't tell the difference.

The wild ones

It's hard today to explain just how huge an impact the movie *The Wild One* had on young people back in the day. It came out in 1953 in the US, and a year or so later here (nothing was as instant as it is today). It starred Marlon Brando, his Triumph motorbike and his anti-everything attitude, and we all wanted to be just like him.

Motorcycle sales took off, and we still buy a huge number of them every year. Mind you, I'm not sure how anyone on a motorcycle survived back then. There were no helmets (they weren't compulsory and looking cool was far more important than being safe), you didn't really have to do anything to pass your licence test except not fall off while some beer-gutted official watched you ride down the street and back, and there was no breathalysing.

booze bus

A police vehicle used to breathalyse drunk drivers and, not as many tourists first believe, a bottle shop on wheels.

cold one

A beer. The amber fluid. The nectar of the gods. Also referred to as a *coldie* or *frothy*. In one of my English beer commercials, I described drinking Foster's as 'like an angel crying on your tongue'.

legless

We have more expressions for throwing up than anything else, though we are hardly short of ways of talking about alcohol. We call it *sauce, plonk, neck oil* or *turps*, as in *a night on the turps*. If you knock back too many beers, you may end up with your pegs not working too well. Which is to say *legless*. Or *blotto*. Or *blind, plastered, hammered*.

stubby

A short bottle of beer, usually 375 ml. The Darwin Stubby, now a rarity, was 2.25 litres. That said a lot about Darwin, and the Northern Territory.

It wasn't until 1968 that New South Wales introduced the breathalyser, a few years after Victoria. Until then almost everyone would drink and drive. It was a bit of a national pastime. Fortunately, of all the risks I took with a motorbike, and there were many, drink-driving, or drink-riding, was never one of them. But I had to share the roads with plenty of people who were soaked, and I no doubt sat in plenty of cars with a drunk driver at the wheel. There was no particular acknowledgement that mixing drinking and driving was a bad thing to do. It was ridiculous we took so long to wake up to it.

Now, I love motorcycles. But you should only be on one if you're under eighteen and think you're immortal. I started riding at sixteen, and, with all the fearlessness and stupidity of an Australian male teenager, I only knew two speeds, stopped and flat out.

Almost everyone would drink and drive. It was a bit of national pastime.

I had a leather jacket with a phoenix painted on the back, a white silk scarf and, doing my darndest to look like Brando, the darkest sunglasses I could find. I had a Triumph like Brando too – mine was a Tiger 100, which cost me $120. Someone had hotted it up before I bought it. It had road-racing gears, an alloy head and quick-lift cams. It could do sixty miles an hour in first gear, so while everyone would beat me off at the lights, they'd be changing into second and I'd still be winding out first. With all that and with the way I dressed, I may as well have had a target on my back and a sign saying: 'Pull me over officer, I'm a two-bob mug lair.'

Close calls

Even without bringing alcohol into the mix, jeez, there were some close calls. One day I was riding through the Royal National Park and, unusually, for me, I was taking it slightly slowly, cruising and looking around. But then an MG sports car roared past me. What?! That was too much!

I tore past the little MG and whipped the Triumph back onto the left side of the road and was still picking up speed when I noticed a tight bend coming up. I laid the bike down to get around it, but this tight bend just kept on bending and the bike slid out from under me and skittered across the road and onto the verge. I stayed on the black stuff, and spun and rolled, and when I finally looked up I was staring directly at an MG bumper bar. It was about eighteen inches from my face.

I should have thanked the driver for pulling up so quickly and saving my life, but I was sixteen.

'Are you okay?' he asked.

It was too early to know, but I immediately said, 'Of course I am,' as if it was no big deal. And then I stood up, shook my shoulders and strutted over to pick up my bike, looking something like the future Leo Wanker and pretending I wasn't humiliated and covered in bruises and gravel rash.

Then there was my somersault. Now that was something. It had been raining heavily in Granville, and I attempted to swing into Victoria Street, where I lived. The bike skidded off the tar and onto the dirt verge, with me still holding on for dear life. There was a dirty big rut waiting for me, and when I hit it the bike kicked up and hurled me right over the fence. It was the six-foot wooden paling fence at the back of the paddock behind the Granville Cinema – an awful old fence that would have done horrible damage if I'd gone into it or landed on top of it. And yet I sailed clean over, like a pole vaulter without a pole, and miraculously landed on my feet on the other side.

So, for once, riding too fast paid off. If I'd been going more slowly I would never have cleared that fence. And my first thought wasn't, *Aren't I lucky to be alive, or at least not filled with a million splinters?* It was: *I'm pissed off that nobody was watching. I could get a job in the circus doing that.*

It's funny, when I look back at my life it's amazing how often I managed to land on my feet. Anyway, on this occasion I had to climb back over the fence to check on my bike. It was as lucky as I was. Just a few scratches on the tank.

So, for once, riding too fast paid off. If I'd been going more slowly I would never have cleared that fence.

A bigger fright came one very dark night while I was hurtling along Heathcote Road, south of the city. I was on my way to the surf club and suddenly my bike's lights went out. It was like someone had put a bag over my head. There were no houses there, so no streetlights, and not even a hint of the moon to help me out. I was doing sixty or seventy miles an hour (in other words, more than a hundred kilometres an hour) and in the pitch black I didn't know if there was a bend coming up, or a cliff or a parked truck.

To this day I don't know how I managed to pull the bike up, still on the road. I sat there completely uninjured but with my heart thumping out of my chest. Then I slowly pushed the bike off the road and hitched a lift.

Later I bought a Triumph Thunderbird, and it was no coincidence that it was the same model Brando rode in the movie. Then a mate and I between us bought a JAP scrambler bike and we tried some dirt-track scrambling over jumps and through water courses. We started with high hopes but never finished a race. I'd like to say the bike kept breaking down, but the problem was talent. Or, to be exact, a lack of it. We kept throwing the bike into the sand.

Still, most of the time riding a motorbike was a great feeling, especially with the wind in your hair in those days before helmets. And amazingly, in all my motorcycling, I never got more than a few bruises. But I was getting into far too much trouble with the constabulary over my antics, and something had to give.

So, when I was drafted in late 1957, I sold my last motorcycle – and probably spent most of the money I received paying off my speeding fines. I never went back to riding bikes, largely because I never went back to being under eighteen and thinking I was immortal.

RIGHT: Queuing at the 'picture palace', this one the famous Roxy in Parramatta.

MOVIE TIME

Like most Australians, I love movies. Though in my case not all movies. I'd be lying if I said I was a huge fan of arthouse cinema. I tend to gravitate towards mainstream fare, be it adventure, comedy or romance. That might be because I was raised largely on American movies and television shows, as were so many Australians. My favourite movie of all time happens to be *Rocky*.

But from the very beginning of the movie industry, Australians have made, and enjoyed, top-notch films of all kinds. Way back in 1906 Aussie director Charles Tait made *The Story of the Kelly Gang*, the first multi-reel, feature-length film produced anywhere in the world. And we've been making wonderful movies ever since, many of which have shaped our culture. My favourites?

Walkabout

This was an odd film, but it showed Australia's outback beautifully, and the performance by David Gulpilil was hypnotic. He'd never acted on screen before that film, yet he stole every scene right up to and including his amazing dance at the end. It was made in 1971 and was the only locally made film from that time that stuck in my mind (though of course it's worth pointing out it had an English director and an English co-star in Jenny Agutter). About fourteen or fifteen years later, we were doing location surveys in Alice Springs for *Crocodile Dundee* and staying at Lasseters Casino, which rather hilariously is named after Lewis Harold Bell Lasseter, a bloke whose delusions about acquiring a pile of gold sent him mad and, eventually, led to him dying alone in the desert. Great ad for playing the tables. Anyway, I had this tap on the shoulder and I swung around. 'G'day Hoges,' David Gulpilil said, and he grinned that grin. I don't know exactly how to describe it, but 'Gulli' and several other Indigenous people I have known, seem to smile with their whole body. I said to myself instantly, 'This bloke has to be in my movie. Gotta have that face lighting up the screen.' So I cast him as Mick Dundee's friend Neville, and his talents were recognised around the world once more.

Mad Max

This was probably the first Australian movie that had an impact in the US. Until then our movies were only shown in small cinemas in other countries. *Mad Max* broke out of that. It was a great action movie by the brilliant Dr George Miller (he's a trained physician too). It showed off our desolate landscape in a scary way no other film had done, and the casting of the soon-to-be megastar Mel Gibson certainly helped (it was 1979, and a very young Mel). Interestingly, though, the voices in *Mad Max* were dubbed for Americans because some pelican of a US studio executive believed no one would understand what the original actors were saying. Didn't seem to matter that Mel was really an American. It put us on our guard for *Dundee* and made us determined not to let them dub our voices. If people couldn't understand what we were saying, bugger 'em, they could go and watch something else. In the end we were partly successful. All the voices stayed the same, but in the US some of the scenes were cut where Australians were talking to one another with no Americans involved. We were told, 'No one wants to hear two Australians talking to one another.'

Babe

A wonderful movie, enchanting. Pure entertainment again from the mind of Dr George Miller. The technology that gave us the talking animals was new and exciting in 1995, though the whole thing made you feel guilty about eating bacon. Most of all, *Babe* just did all the good things a movie can do. I believe you get more out of a movie than you do out of any book or radio show or podcast, because it's visual and aural and you turn up in a mindset to be entertained.

The Castle

There was a survey in early 2022 to choose the most Australian film ever. *Crocodile Dundee* was second behind *The Castle* – and quite rightly so. *Crocodile Dundee* was an attempt to make a movie that would work outside Australia by pushing the image that the other people had of us. *The Castle*, from 1997, was pure local entertainment, which no one else could properly understand. With the version shown overseas, by the time they'd changed references to rissoles and *Hey Hey It's Saturday* and various types of Holden, it had lost a bit of its magic. But the original version, for us, was special from start to finish. The script, with its now famous lines – 'What do you call this?'; 'It's the vibe of it, it's the constitution, it's Mabo, it's justice'; 'This is going straight to the pool room'; etc – and its wonderful cast (it's surely Michael Caton's best performance) all just clicked and created magic.

CHAPTER 7

Larrikins, Rogues and Mates

The most colourful characters of all

The original larrikins hung around The Rocks, which was the oldest and most dangerous part of Sydney. They carried knives and clubs. They robbed people, they were bad news, the gangsters of their era. Modern larrikins, I'm pleased to say, are a better breed. They do without the knives, violence and crime. But they still have a healthy suspicion of authority and love to stir things up.

There is something Americans call 'sticking it to the man'. Australians have always done that, probably because the man was originally a prison guard or magistrate. Our modern larrikins are essentially lovable rogues, mischievous characters who enjoy a bit of fun and don't take life or themselves too seriously.

They adhere to the Australian principle of mateship – staying loyal to your friends, an idea that really took hold during World War I, when loyalty and mutual support among Anzac troops were potentially lifesaving and therefore heroic. Larrikinism is still seen as a distinctive and treasured Australian trait, and aspiring to be at least a bit of a larrikin, I reckon, is part of our deepest nature. That's why so many of the people we admire most are larrikins. In what other country could a bloke like Bob Hawke become not just prime minister, but the most popular one ever?

The larrikin spirit

Australian history is dotted with larrikins and rogues, probably due to our dubious beginnings. There were also more than a few ratbags along the way, another fact probably directly related to our dubious beginnings. If nothing else, this abundance of dodgy types has given us a wide range of terms of abuse for those in charge, and has contributed to our peculiar sense of humour.

How to Speak 'STRAYAN

larrikin

A mischievous character; someone who is anti-authoritarian and likes to cause a bit of trouble, without doing any great harm. Can also be used as an adjective, as in *a larrikin bloke*, *the larrikin spirit*.

Samuel Marsden, the 'flogging parson of Parramatta'. Handing out severe punishment didn't put him off his food, if this portrait is any indication.

Early ratbags

A prime example of a ratbag from the convict era is Samuel Marsden. He was born in Yorkshire in 1765 and moved to Sydney in 1794, where he built a home near Parramatta, not far from my old stomping grounds. His bio calls him a 'chaplain, missionary, farmer and magistrate', but it was as a magistrate – and an utter tyrant of a magistrate – that he is best remembered. He was the sort of guy who would sentence people to hundreds of lashes, and they'd die from the flogging, or he'd then hang them. And he was a man of the cloth. That's how cruel the convict era could be.

Another relic of that horrible time is the 'Female Factory'. The building is still in Parramatta, in the same park as Cumberland Oval. I'd go to the footy there and then walk past this one-time cruel, overcrowded prison and workhouse for young girls, and wonder what ratbag thought it was a good

I never quite understood why Ned Kelly was a hero. Then again, I never understood how you can have a beard like that and not be reminded of last week's pie and sauce. This photograph was taken just before his execution in 1880.

idea, and just how much misery has been contained within those brick walls.

In Victoria, in the second half of the nineteenth century, we had Ned Kelly. The UK had Robin Hood, the US had Billy the Kid, and we had this dopey guy who robbed banks with a bucket on his noggin. Yeah, there was a bit of ingenuity in making his own armour, and a bit of theatre in having a gang all in the same dress-ups, so you can have a sneaking admiration for him. But at the same time, he's not much of a national role model.

In 1878 Ned and his gang were involved in the Stringybark Creek shootings, in which three policemen died. Like Errol Flynn, later, Ned Kelly was very aware of his image and told a few whoppers in support of it too. He manipulated the public into thinking he was some kind of hero, protecting his class, defending his mother and all that, and it suited a country in search of symbols to believe him. He was a crook, but he was standing up to the man, so you had to get behind him.

Ned ended up on the end of a rope, but stayed a hero to many nonetheless.

Errol the Tasmanian devil

In 1909 an elegant, well-respected, educated couple in Hobart gave birth to a boy they described as a little angel. He rapidly turned out to be a Tasmanian devil.

Mr and Mrs Flynn called their son Errol, and he would go on to become the most famous Australian of his time, and one of the most famous people in the world. As a screen actor, he was the equivalent of Tom Cruise and Brad Pitt rolled into one, the biggest, most dashing movie star of the 1940s and 1950s.

A lot of Errol's backstory can't be authenticated, as he was a pretty big yarn-spinner and there weren't a lot of people taking notes during his less reputable exploits. He was somewhere between a lovable larrikin, by his own account (in the book *My Wicked, Wicked Ways*), and a nasty piece of work, according to others.

How to Speak 'STRAYAN

flash as a rat with a gold tooth

Refers to someone having airs and graces when they haven't earnt them, or don't deserve them. You're a rat – what are you doing with a gold tooth? It's a great expression, and I think it came from Australian writer Frank Hardy. Not to be confused with *as cunning as a shithouse rat*, which means ... well, that one's pretty obvious.

He was certainly a villainous kid and after he got kicked out of several schools, much to the horror of his parents, he decided – he later explained – that the little isle of Tasmania was too boring for him. At seventeen he signed on as a deckhand and sailed to Sydney. He hung around The Rocks and got in with the original larrikins, known as the Rocks Push. A push was a gang, in the language of the time, and the Rocks Push was a notoriously dangerous one.

He ran afoul of the police and, rather than go in for questioning, signed on to another ship that sailed up to New Guinea. He met the same type of dodgy people, and got into the same type of trouble. He claimed that he shot someone dead but was acquitted because it was in self-defence.

Quite a lot of Errol Flynn's autobiography was coloured in, shall we say. He claimed to have hopped onto another ship, this time as captain. It's possible that he was captain; he could have certainly charmed someone into promoting him. He and his crew sailed across the Pacific and ran into Australian film director Charles Chauvel and his crew in Tahiti. It was 1933, and they were in the process

Granville Cinema in 1942, the year Gentleman Jim *came out. Errol Flynn played heavyweight champion James J. Corbett, so as a fan of Errol and boxing, I was doubly hooked years later when I finally saw the movie at this very cinema.*

of making *In the Wake of the Bounty*, the first film about the mutiny on the *Bounty*.

When Errol turned up with his swagger, his good looks and his charm, Chauvel decided to cast this unknown Tasmanian as Fletcher Christian. And when people in Hollywood saw the rough footage, the thing they noticed was that this strikingly handsome, manly-looking guy had so much charisma he stole every scene. So they grabbed hold of him and signed him up for their movies. He appeared in *Captain Blood* as the pirate-ship captain, Peter Blood, typecast totally, because Errol was a bit of a pirate. Then he was Robin Hood in *The Adventures of Robin Hood*, another good bit of casting, though I don't think Errol ever gave much back to the poor.

The Cinema and The Castle were the two Granville picture houses, and The Cinema was only two hundred yards

How to Speak 'STRAYAN

pants man

The polite term is *ladies' man*, but *pants man* is so much better. You still hear it a lot.

from the back of my place. When Errol Flynn came on the screen, there was a collective gush from the girls, but we liked him too. He had so much presence. He was not only handsome, but heroic.

We were proud too because he was an Aussie. It was in the era of, you know, Cary Grant, John Wayne, those kind of guys, but the man's man, the swashbuckler's swashbuckler, was Errol Flynn. When you saw him in *Captain Blood* and *The Adventures of Robin Hood* you knew no one should have played those parts after him.

In terms of being a pants man, he claimed every day of his life he set out to bed a different woman, and, according to him, he rarely failed. We now know some of them were very young. Oh yeah, Errol was questionable. And as if to prove a lot of his stories about his adventures and hard living were true, he ended up a bloated drunk and died at fifty.

A lot of Errol's backstory can't be authenticated, as he was a pretty big yarn-spinner and there weren't a lot of people taking notes during his less reputable exploits.

When South Sydney won the 1971 Rugby League Grand Final, their captain and famous hard man John Sattler was carried by a teammate for a victory lap.

Johnny Sattler, the toughest of the lot

Johnny 'Satts' Sattler was one of the hard men of sport, any sport. He played for Australia in rugby league and famously had his jaw broken in two places by a punch when captaining the South Sydney Rabbitohs in the 1970 Sydney Grand Final. You were only allowed to replace one player back then, so Sattler wasn't going to let his team down over such a minor matter. He kept playing for the next seventy minutes and helped them win a famous victory.

While on that occasion someone managed to land a good punch on him, it was often the other way around. He was sent off for foul play fifteen times in his career, and you had to do a hell of a lot more back then to get sent off. Even the bloke who broke Johnny's jaw didn't get his marching orders. Those things were just part of the game.

When I was starting out in television, I was asked to do various fundraisers, and I was always happy to help out. One time I was roped into a charity camel race at Redfern Oval, the home of Satts's legendary Rabbitohs rugby league team. I'd never ridden a camel before, so I was very gently making my way around the footy field, trying to get the hang of it.

A couple of the Souths players were also nervously working out how to handle their camels, and I noticed the man himself – Johnny Sattler – standing by, watching us all.

So, I'm finely balanced way up on top of this camel, holding on for dear life, because although there was a saddle, there were no reins. And Johnny Sattler walks up, produces a stick out of nowhere and whacks my camel in the nuts. Needless to say, the thing goes troppo and throws me clean off.

It's a long way down from a camel, but somehow, as usual, I land on my feet. I'm still holding handfuls of hair and I'm in shock, but, as I watch Sattler running away giggling, the red mist comes down. 'You bastard!' I yell.

I sprint after him but, after a few steps, I stop. It's Johnny Sattler, for Chrissakes. What the hell am I going to do if I catch him? This guy could tear my head off without raising a sweat. Could probably do it even with a broken jaw and a dislocated shoulder.

So I stand my ground and yell out, laughing: 'That was really funny, getting me hurled off a camel.'

Yeah, Satts was as big and tough and hard as you could possibly be. The absolute toughest one of the lot.

The Captain in full 'man about town' mode.

Hunting elephants with the Captain

Some people are both larrikins *and* rogues. Captain Peter Janson is a good example of what you might call a lovable rogue – if you can love a big, bearded man with a fondness for cravats, smoking jackets and deer-stalker hats.

The Captain was a well-known man-about-town in Melbourne from, I guess, the late 1960s. I met him in the 1970s and he was great company, a thrower of huge parties and a teller of many tales.

He described himself as a 'gentleman'. He claimed to be related to royalty, the black sheep of some branch of the British Royal Family that was big in the Indian Raj. But it was all front. As far as anyone could discover, he was a New Zealand farm boy who had arrived in Melbourne via England. The Captain was always rushing off overseas, supposedly to play chukkers with

Prince Charlie or to shoot tigers in Bengal with his dear friend, the Sultan of Baroda.

He said it was the Bhutanese Army that had awarded him the title of Captain, but I think he said that only after the British Army told him to stop claiming his title had anything to do with them. Janson raced cars too, and he'd say, 'Rev rev,' when he shook your hand, in case you forgot. Wasn't a bad driver actually, but his real talent was being Peter Janson.

He somehow convinced the owners of the Hotel Windsor to give him access to the attic, which was several linked rooms, as his bachelor pad. In it, he had an amazing collection of what he called treasures. He'd point to, say, a shitty old guitar and say, 'John Lennon gave me that.' Everything came with a story, everything was somehow related to someone famous or some important battle, or came from a castle or stately home where the Captain had connections.

He'd ring me up and say, 'I've got Don Lane and Bert Newton coming over for dinner on the weekend and they are both very keen that you join us.' The first time he did this, I said, 'Yeah, all right.' Then he'd ring Don and say, 'I've got Paul Hogan and Bert Newton coming over for dinner on the weekend and they are both very keen that you join us.' And then he'd ring Bert with the same spiel, and then he'd get onto his business contacts and tell them he had all these influential Channel 9 people coming over for a bit of a turn-out, and it would be really good exposure for their brand if they supplied the Champagne, or caviar, or fine wines or whatever it was that they sold. The vans would start turning up with the cartons of grog and plates of oysters or whatever. He was a consistently colourful character.

'We were meant to be hunting elephants together, but one of your manservants turned up and said you'd gone ahead with the Maharaja!'

The Hotel Windsor was sold and the new owners finally managed to kick Janson out, but he turned up again in some big flash warehouse. Whose it was, no one knew. I was filming the *Anzacs* miniseries nearby and there was a delay, so I took a few of the crew and actors with me to crash the Captain's new and even bigger bachelor pad, hear his stories and be plied with alcohol and caviar obtained by dubious means. 'The Captain'd love to meet you,' I said to the blokes, but when we got there, there was a security detail on the door, which was a joke in itself, and the pelican in charge said I could come in, but not my mates.

I told the *Anzacs* guys to wait outside and I burst into the big loungeroom where Janson was regaling about half a dozen people with the usual tall tales. 'You bastard!' I shouted. 'Where were you?'

'What?' Janson looked at me, not quite sure what was going on.

'We were meant to be hunting elephants together, but one of your manservants turned up and said you'd gone ahead with the Maharaja!'

His facial expression changed completely. 'Oh, Paul, I'm so sorry. His Excellency was getting impatient. But I hope my palatial suite made up for it.'

I could see his face bursting with nothing short of love. I had backed up his utter nonsense about always being off with royalty or some other stuffed shirts, and he was suddenly about a foot taller. All my *Anzacs* mates were now welcome – the whole flaming platoon as far as he was concerned – and, as we'd hoped, we spent the evening being plied with tall tales, alcohol and caviar.

I always imagined that if Errol Flynn hadn't fluked a film career, he might have talked his way into living at the top of the Hotel Windsor, thrown parties and lured women up there with liquor and outrageous tales.

Bush whackers

Among this country's most colourful characters and biggest delights are dry-witted bastards from the bush. These are creatures all of their own, characters who haven't changed a bit in a couple of hundred years (it seems) and still embody the larrikin spirit. You can't help but smile when you meet them.

In the late 1970s or thereabouts, we were driving to Gulargambone which, aside from anything else, is one of the best place names in the world. It's between Dubbo and Walgett in central New South Wales, and we were heading there to do a cigarette commercial in a shearing shed. We saw this ute on the side of the road, with the bonnet up, and we pulled alongside and offered to help. The crusty old farmer standing there said, 'No use, mate, it's completely knackered.'

'We'll give you a lift then. We're going into Gulargambone.'

He said, 'No use, mate, I'm going to Bullagreen. That's where the action is.'

There were only about three or four hundred people living in Gulargambone at that time, and I'm not sure if there

'When I see you on the TV, you're surrounded by sheilas. You got none here.'

was anyone at all living in Bullagreen. But when a guy like that delivers such a deadpan line, you never know if he's taking the mick, or if all the action really is in Bullagreen.

Sometime later when we were all set up to film the commercial, the bloke who owned the property, who was well into his sixties, said, 'My dad wants to come down and have a peek.' Sure enough, his dad came down. He looked exactly the same, only older and more tanned and windblown. The first thing he said was, 'Is the boy looking after you?', even though his 'boy' was probably sixty-five. Then he said, 'Where's the sheilas?'

'What do you mean?' I asked.

'When I see you on the TV, you're surrounded by sheilas. You got none here.'

This bloke was in his late eighties, and when he realised there were no sheilas, he was off.

Country pranks

A lot of these great old Aussies are a complicated lot. I remember friends and rellos of my dad all loved the Queen and would never swear in front of a woman. But in other ways they were completely wild, absolute dead-set larrikins.

An old family friend of my dad's, Roy, was the classic example. If a man swore within earshot of a member of the fairer sex – and 'fairer sex' is how he would have put it – Roy was likely to give him a clip around the ears, or simply flatten him. It was okay for a woman to see that apparently, but not to

It's a different world out there in the bush! It gives us some of our most eccentric characters and driest wits. They don't mind a drink or a prank, either.

hear a dirty word. One night before cars were common, Roy, who wasn't much of a dancer, went to the local hall that was holding the yearly Belle of the Ball dance.

Once everyone was inside safely dancing the night away, Roy got their horses and carts, unhooked them, then placed the horses on one side of the nearby fence, the carts on the other and reconnected them. The revellers wandered out at 2 a.m. to find their horses and carts standing there safely, but now with a fence going through them. Everyone looked skywards and cried 'Roy!'

Another time when Roy was living in the country, a new neighbour was about to spend his first night in an old house that stood about half a mile away in a secluded paddock. Roy waited for the man to leave the house then sneaked over, messed

hoon

A lout. The words *hoon* and *larrikin* used to have sinister connotations, but *hoon* hasn't been rehabilitated in the same way as *larrikin*. Being a hoon is not a positive. Your best mates might be larrikins, but hoons are the dickheads doing burnouts in their hotted-up cars and yelling at people.

up his sheets and put a pair of old false teeth in a glass of water beside his bed. The new neighbour arrived home and was soon convinced there was someone still living in his new house. He was so scared he spent the night sleeping in his truck.

Sporting chancer

But my favourite character was an old bushy from Mitta Mitta in north-east Victoria called Felix Lumby. Felix was a classic poacher, always sneaking around the rivers without a fishing licence and prepared to adopt whatever methods necessary, legal or not, to catch as many fish as he could. Drum-nets, set lines and gelignite were all part of his fishing kit. I actually borrowed the geligniting fish technique for the opening scene of *Dundee II*.

For those lucky enough to not know what this is, it's the practice of basically letting a bomb off under the water so it stuns the fish and they float to the surface. Not very sporting, but it didn't stop people like Felix from spruiking his fishing prowess to all and sundry. One night he was in the local pub, bragging to the whole room that he had caught over thirty fish that very afternoon. Suddenly a stranger stepped forward and asked, 'Do you know who I am?' Felix said no, and the man announced, 'I'm the new fishing inspector.'

'Well, do you know who I am?' Felix shot back without missing a beat. The inspector shook his head, and Felix said, 'I'm the biggest bullshit artist in this whole valley!'

Nature got its revenge on poor Felix though. You see, fish weren't the only thing he went after with dynamite. He also used it to keep down the rabbit population. He was a master in the barbaric and unsportsmanlike ritual of using a ferret to catch a rabbit, then blocking all the holes coming out of the rabbit's warren, strapping a stick of dynamite to the captured rabbit and sending it back down the burrow. Obviously the burrow and everything in it would be blown sky high.

bluey

A nickname Australians give to people with red hair. It came about, I believe, because people with red hair were assumed to be Irish, and the Irish were assumed to be fiery or hot-tempered, and likely to start a fight at any moment. And a fight was *a blue*. We had two redheads in our Harbour Bridge rugby league team, and both were called Bluey. There was Bluey Lawson and Bluey Seymour. Now, Bluey Seymour was a classic example of what we called a club stalwart. That meant a guy who'd played too long, and was usually balding and overweight. We stuck Bluey Seymour in the front row, where being overweight and having a rough head was an advantage. The games were at the Reg Bartley Oval at Rushcutters Bay down on the harbour. When we came off at half-time, we'd run through the crowd of family and friends into the dressing room. And I'd love going behind Bluey Seymour because his missus would always be standing there as we ran through, holding out an open tinnie and a lit cigarette for him. Bluey would grab them on the trot, like a marathon runner reaching for his paper cup of water, and stumble into the changeroom. He'd be completely exhausted after a gruelling first half, but with his durrie and his cold one, he'd be all set for the ten-minute break and would be able to get back up and give it his all in the second half. As you can tell from that, we were obviously not first-graders. With no disrespect, the competition was for hasbeens and neverwasers, but we won the premiership in our first season. And a fair bit of the credit has to go to Bluey's missus.

The fun bit is that one particular day all was going according to plan when suddenly, from about fifty metres away, Felix saw the loaded rabbit's head bob up out of a hole. This was a big burrow, a bloody big burrow, and not all the holes had been plugged. So the rabbit came out, ran across the paddock and shot right under Felix's new Land Rover. The really tough one with the fold-down windscreen, the one that is built to withstand anything. Well, almost anything. *Kaboom!*

Underdogs are heroes too

We Australians have always had a deep respect for the sort of person who bites off more than they can chew, then keeps chomping away. Yep, the underdog has always been right up there in that hallowed pantheon of Australian favourites. Take the aforementioned incompetent explorers Robert O'Hara Burke and William John Wills. They became more famous and revered than a whole lot of explorers who were actually very good at the job.

Burke and Wills led a party to make the first transcontinental crossing from Adelaide to Darwin. Even though they were badly prepared and doomed from the start, Australians admired that they dared to go to the centre and have a look around. We were fascinated by the centre because we all lived on the fringes.

Okay, so Burke and Wills left in 1860, discovered not much more than a whole lot of inhospitable land, and were dead by 1861, but they'd gone out and had a red-hot go. That made them underdogs, and we can all get behind that particular breed of canine.

The departure of the Burke and Wills expedition – into the desert and into legend. It says something about Australia that Burke and Wills became much better known than explorers who knew what they were doing.

FAVOURITE DEAD-SET
CHEEKY BUGGERS

I've made the point that to be an Australian, you have to have a little bit of larrikin in you. Here are some cheeky buggers who had a lot of it in them and loved to take the mickey out of everyone and everything.

Dawn Fraser

There was a time when we didn't want female larrikins. We called women 'sheilas' and wanted them to be well behaved, know their place, and be pretty to look at. And then came champion swimmer Dawn Fraser.

She was a strong, bold woman who was going to do and say whatever she wanted. If anyone called her out, she could simply hold up a handful of gold medals. Or just biff 'em, or sometimes maybe both. And we thought, *Hey that's pretty good, we could come to like this.*

Dawn Fraser was the greatest swimmer of her generation. She won eight Olympic medals (including four golds) across Sydney, Rome and Tokyo, and set a string of world records, some of which stood for years and years. Her antics, whether refusing to wear the official Olympic swimming costume or telling officials what she really thought of them, saw her banned and condemned and pilloried, yet she shrugged it all off. At the 1964 Olympics in Tokyo, she supposedly swam the moat at the emperor's palace to steal an imperial flag. That made us like her even more – particularly since she managed to charm the Japanese police so much they let her keep the flag and bring it back as a souvenir.

Germaine Greer

When feminism swept the world, including God's own country down here, there were three bibles for the movement.

And although we had a reputation as a misogynistic country – and in some ways we were – we did produce the author of one of those bibles, Germaine Greer.

What's more, *The Female Eunuch* was the only one of the three books with any humour in it. Germaine is one of the smartest people you'll ever meet, and among the most fearless, outspoken and outrageous. Imposing too: Germaine with heels on – she wore them for a scene-stealing appearance in *Hogan in London* – is about six foot three.

David Boon

A great cricketer, a great character and a great athlete. He must have been, as in 1989 he drank fifty-two cans of Victoria Bitter on a flight to England then immediately fronted up for The Ashes. That drinking feat equated to 19.5 litres of beer in 24 hours. The story goes that the Qantas captain announced it on the PA, telling the passengers that Boon had comfortably set a new record of fifty-two tinnies, eclipsing the shared record of forty-four attributed to Australia's wicketkeeper Rod Marsh and batsman Doug Walters.

Boonie was a really good cricketer, yet fifty-two tinnies not out is the only stat of his that anyone remembers. So I should add here that Australia won that Ashes series four to zip, and Boon scored 442 runs at 55.25. The Tasmanian is really good company too, larger than life. No surprise that VB picked him up as a brand ambassador. No one could say he didn't love the product.

Bob Hawke

Australians tend to judge a male politician by whether he might be a good bloke to have a beer with. There was probably no bloke better to have a beer with – or several beers with – than Bob Hawke. He was a man of many talents. He was a Rhodes Scholar and a brilliant speaker, a very smart and educated man in every sense. But he wasn't looked up to for that so much as the fact he was a mug punter and held a couple of drinking records. At one stage he made

The Guinness Book of World Records for sculling a yard glass of ale in eleven seconds. A yard is two-and-a-half pints, or 1.4 litres. He was a half-decent cricketer too.

Hawke got into quite a bit of strife in public life, and in the marital game. Yet his stocks kept rising. When I was in my first TV job, as the resident comic on *A Current Affair*, I'd sometimes do joke interviews with politicians and bigwigs. I interviewed Hawkie, who was then head of the ACTU, the Australian Council of Trade Unions, and I asked him jokingly if he thought he should be prime minister. He said, yeah, he wouldn't mind having a go at running the place.

I was no journalist and thought his comment was just part of a fun conversation. But the show's host, Mike Willesee, was over the moon. He thought I'd landed a great scoop: Bob Hawke finally admits he wants to be PM. About ten years later, Bob Hawke *was* PM. And in a country known for giving its PMs the flick real quick, he held on to the top job for nearly nine years.

I was sad to see Hawkie leave The Lodge, the prime ministerial residence in Canberra. The whole country was. He and I stayed in contact. In early 2019 I went around to his place to have a drink and a chat. He was doing the crossword – we both loved a crossword puzzle – and I looked over and could see the answer to one clue he hadn't got. I leant forward to point it out. But even in his late eighties, Hawkie had enough mongrel in him to thump my hand right out of the way. I totally understood that, because I'm the same: shut up, don't tell me the answer.

When I went home, I thought, *Wow, there we were, two older blokes arguing over a crossword.* Yet he'd been the Australian prime minister. Hawkie died a couple of months later, and there was a huge outpouring of grief and affection from the Australian public.

I ran into a few other Australian PMs, though none had the larrikin streak of Hawkie. I interviewed John Gorton for *A Current Affair* on the rooftop of a fancy hotel and he was sitting down having a beer and just talking. He dropped cigarette ash in his beer and said, 'Oh, it's all right,' and kept on drinking it. That showed some of his character: he wasn't fussy, he didn't waste things. Some ash in his beer wasn't going to worry John Gorton. Mind you, he must have been made of pretty strong stuff. He'd had half his face torn off in the war and, while he was being evacuated to safety straight afterwards, his boat was torpedoed by a Japanese submarine.

People think of Billy McMahon, who replaced him, as a bit of buffoon now, but when I ended up sitting next to him at a dinner he was friendly and chatty, which was a pleasant surprise because I'd mocked him on television. His wife was a different story. Lady Sonia was annoyed at Billy having a chat with me. She thought I was well beneath the likes of them.

Gough Whitlam, who replaced McMahon, was progressive politically, but posh. I never thought of him as one of the boys. But he did all right, I guess. Brought in big changes. At one point there was a fundraiser in Melbourne where we both appeared.

He went up first and delivered this speech plugging himself and his party with great earnestness and quite a bit of pomposity. I couldn't help myself. I picked up a broom and sneaked onto the back of the stage while he was still talking. I started sweeping and the crowd erupted, but Gough never looked around.

Even when the crowd was roaring, he thought it was all about him. I remember John Cornell saying, 'Now there's a man on good terms with himself.'

cobber

A great mate. Maybe this classic Australian word was invented in the army; it was certainly used by diggers in the trenches. Some say it is from the Yiddish word *chaber*, meaning comrade, which may have arrived here with the convicts from London's East End. Others argue it's from the word *cob* which, in some regional English dialect means to take a liking to someone.

mate

A great friend. Perhaps the greatest single Australian word, and one not used anywhere else in quite the same way. In America you call someone *pal*, but it's usually a negative, really, as in 'Watch it, pal.' The rhyming slang version of *mate* is *china plate*. 'Thanks, China!'

mate's rates

A discount because you know someone. When I lived at Chullora there was a guy across the road who loved a bargain. His name was Jack and you could hardly walk through his house for all the refrigerators and freezers and other things in there that he'd managed to snag on the cheap. Once he got a special deal from someone he knew on three Simca car engines. They were brand new, in the box, and Jack was so pleased with himself. No idea what he was going to do with them though. One day he turned up at our place wearing a lady's wig. He'd bought a whole box of them. 'They only cost me two dollars,' he explained, smiling like he'd won the lottery.

Mates and mateship

Mateship is every bit as important today in Australia as it ever was. It's a big part of our makeup, one of the backbones of our egalitarian society. The tourists of 1788 were the lowest of the low, and lorded over by cruel guards. So they had to stick together. It was us against the system. And then when we went overseas to wars, as we did regularly, it was us against the enemy and sometimes, us against the British officers who thought we were merely cannon fodder. From all this came the idea of the *fair go*, a determination not to reproduce the British class structure Down Under, and the distinctively Australian concept of mateship.

There are mates, and there are mates. I've had some great ones at every stage of my life. But there was one mate who stood head and shoulders above all the rest.

John 'Corny' Cornell – my best mate

The great mate in my life was John Cornell (1941–2021). I've said many times I would have taken a bullet for him, and I'm sure he would have taken one for me. Yet when we met, there was little that was common in our backgrounds. He was so worldly and sophisticated, and I knew nothing about anything really, and certainly nothing about my new industry, television. But we hit it off immediately.

I thought I'd need to be a bit fancy when I was on the box, to seem a bit more worldly or well read, and John told me to forget that, to just go for it as if I was addressing my mates at the pub. He said, 'You are here because you are a blue-collar worker in Australia, and none of us TV people have experienced what that's like.'

Despite our differences, we had the same larrikin spirit. When I needed a dopey sidekick for a skit, this smart, well-spoken, good-looking guy was perfectly happy to go on national television with a lifesaver's hat on, pull a strange face and act like an idiot. And he was perfectly happy to be named Strop, a *stropper* being a wanker.

He got comedy straight away, much like he picked up everything else. He knew instinctively if you do comedy, you can't do it out of vanity. If it requires you to look grotesque, or something ridiculous, you just do it.

Corny was a dead-set cricket fan. We were both sports lovers. We could talk our heads off, or say nothing for half an hour. Mates don't have to try to impress each other. They just enjoy each other's company. We could trust each other without question. I'd have nothing but good thoughts for him, and vice versa.

Corny and I set out on a hell of an adventure together. Mike Willesee and Clyde Packer, my early managers, talked at one stage about sticking me on a quiz show with some other people, but John had much bigger ambitions for me. He convinced everyone that I should have my very own television show. That sounded like madness, even to me. But he made it work.

I remember him doing an interview and being asked if it was Corny who wrote my material. 'What I do is sharpen his pencils and correct the spelling mistakes,' he said. 'It's coming out of his head. Not mine.' That was his usual modesty, completely downplaying how important he was in the mix.

Everything I wrote was too long and John was the perfect subeditor. As anyone in the business will tell you, the difference between fair, good and great can all be in the edit. John knew exactly which bits needed to go. And he wrote all the stuff for his own character, Strop, of course.

John had many skills. He was a brilliant entrepreneur and when he could see potential in something – almost anything – he could immediately work out what needed to be done to make it better. Whether it was television shows or movies, sporting competitions or businesses, my best mate had the gift.

Best of mates: me and Corny. Delvene, centre, said our friendship was 'as tender and loving as a relationship between two straight ex-boxers could ever be'.

Corny and I were like brothers, and we did so much together. I wrote *Crocodile Dundee* out as a story in my usual block letters and then Corny and I shared an Oscar nomination (with Ken Shadie) for the screenplay. Who could have imagined that would happen to a couple of knockabout mates who'd never made a film before? Corny produced *Crocodile Dundee* too, and I had him produce and direct *Crocodile Dundee II* and *Almost an Angel*. Being John, he did a fantastic job.

But after that, he started to fade. He had Parkinson's, though we didn't know it at the time. He just wasn't up to things, didn't have the fire that had enabled him to do so much, from directing movies, to developing Australia's finest pubs, to thinking up World Series Cricket for Kerry Packer.

Corny was sick for over twenty years. I was living in LA, but he flew over and visited me when he could, and I'd fly back and stay with him and his lovely wife, Dele – actress Delvene Delaney, who was a regular in *The Paul Hogan Show* – and we'd just hang out. I wish I could have done more for him, particularly when I think about what he did for me. He changed my life completely. Opened the world up for me.

There's nothing more Australian than mateship. And if you get just one mate as good as John in your life, you're very lucky. We were mates for fifty years.

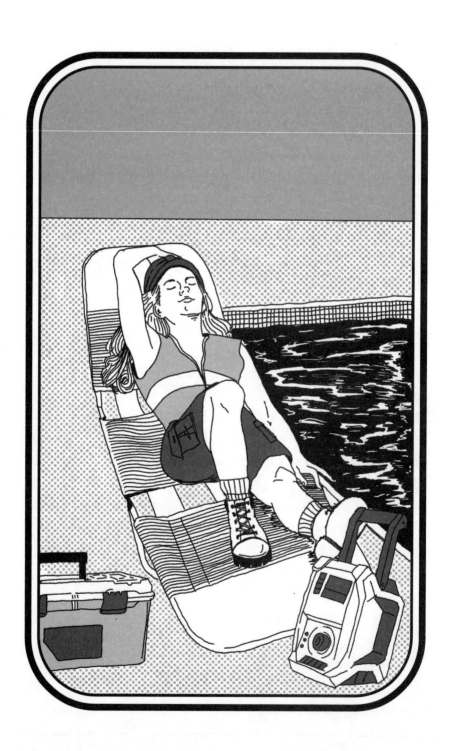

CHAPTER 8

We're Not Perfect But ...

All in all, Australia's not bad, and here's why

A mate – a very rude mate – recently said I'm turning into an action figure of myself. It's true that I've shrunk. I'm an inch and a half shorter, and twenty pounds lighter than back in the day. And while I've been going backwards, everyone else has been racing ahead. For most of my life, I was around five nine, or about 175 centimetres. That was considered average height. I never thought of myself as tall or short, but the world has moved on – and up. I keep seeing teenage girls who are more than six feet tall. I look at my grandchildren and their friends, and it's Land of the Giants.

I might be an ever-smaller fish in a bigger pond, but I keep a close watch on everything around me with great interest. And I have nothing but confidence in the people of

Australia and the way this country is heading. Just wish I could be around for another fifty or so years to see it!

We can toss out our government

Australia had seven changes of PM between 2007 and 2022, but that's not a weakness. It's a strength.

Australians were never going to put up with being ruled by kings or emperors or shahs, or grand poobahs or presidents-for-life. We liked having the Queen come out to raise money for charity and open fêtes and things like that, but we're never going to obey if she suggests something we don't want to do.

We leant more towards the American thing: government of the people, by the people, for the people. But we improved on that in many ways. We don't have to put up with some galah for four years. As soon as they annoy us, or don't do what we want, we kick them out – or we get our elected representatives to do it on our behalf.

We say, 'We don't like the way you're doing the job. There, you go, we're getting someone else.'

No one else on the planet does that so fast. I think this is the only country in the world that has changed its leadership so often without whoever's holding the reins having committed a serious crime and without the country spilling a single drop of blood. Our leaders may whinge and whine when they get the chop, but they basically say, 'I'm not happy about it, but it's a fair cop and I'll go quietly.'

A lot of Americans loved Trump because they thought he was a billionaire, whereas I can't imagine Australians voting in someone like that. When John Hewson was our opposition leader, the media just couldn't get beyond the fact that he had a Ferrari in the shed. It was mentioned in every story.

People whinge about our political system and I say, 'Try living somewhere else, if you think this is crook.' A lot of other countries are stuck with some sort of inherited boofheaded leadership for decades, and systems that don't work. Look at North Korea. In fact, look at Western countries and compare, say, our education systems. In England, education is run at least partly along class lines. In America it's not a class system, it's a money system. The black districts don't get good schools, and in many of the poorer white areas, the same is true. And if you can pull yourself up by the bootstraps and go to college, it's going to be bloody expensive. You often hear of people struggling for years or even decades to pay off their college loans. Here, uni is much cheaper and you usually pay it off via HECS – the Higher Education Compensation Scheme – which means you pay a bit more tax, but much later on, and only when you're earning a decent sum. Much smarter.

We can see a doctor for free – and soon

Likewise, people put down the health system in Australia, but you don't want to get sick anywhere else. I've been in hospital in the UK and I've been in hospital a couple of times in the US. The Americans are always saying they have the best medical system in the world, and they certainly have fabulous doctors and facilities for the well off. But in Australia, you go to hospital even if you don't have a brass razoo. Same is true in the UK, but you join the queue trying to get in if you're a non-paying guest: 'Oh yes, we'll look after you, just come back in seven or eight weeks.' Here people can get medical attention when they need it. And it's world-class. I'm not saying what the Yanks and Poms have isn't, but you usually have to wait in the UK and, if you don't have a lot of money in the US, you might have to mortgage your house to pay for your care. *Breaking Bad* wouldn't have happened here. A school teacher with lung cancer wouldn't need to cook crystal meth. We'd have just said to Walter White, 'Chuck us across your Medicare card, sport, and Bob's your uncle.'

Everyone's a comedian

While we have a long history of great Aussie comics and comedians, no one is funnier than our funniest mate. We all have one. The guy or girl who makes us laugh more than anyone. They might be a butcher or a hairdresser or whatever, but they are better than anyone who has ever appeared on the idiot box.

I was watching the news about the Queensland floods in 2010 and they were interviewing an old guy (someone my age) who was standing in three feet of water.

'Is there much damage to your house?' asked the reporter.

'Dunno, we haven't found it yet.'

On another occasion, a reporter from overseas asked an Australian farmer, 'Have you lived your whole life in Queensland?' The farmer replied, 'Not yet.'

I met dozens of these types on the great road trip we made while shooting *Charlie & Boots* in 2008. We travelled from Warrnambool, in southern Victoria, all the way to the Top End of Australia and met wonderful characters every step of the way. If you've never left the city, you should. There's a whole continent full of people and entertainment out there.

We stopped in Weethalle in the Central West of New South Wales, a town in the middle of nowhere with nothing but a few bored cows and a couple of dogs making up the numbers. I saw a little café, walked in and asked the old bloke behind the counter if I could have a cappuccino. He looked at me and drily said, 'Where do you think you are?'

'Have you lived your whole life in Queensland?'
'Not yet.'

Weethalle is in NSW's Bland Shire, though the people are anything but, as I learned in the local café.

'But you've got it written up on your board,' I replied. 'Right there – it says cappuccino.'

'Yeah, but the machine's been broken for five or six years, hasn't it?'

Obviously, this was new information to me, so I reconsidered and said, no worries, I'd have a cup of tea instead.

'I thought you wanted a cappuccino?'

Now I was really confused. He said his missus had a mixer that frothed the milk and she'd make me one. He walked to the little gap that separated the café from their residence and sang out, 'Doris! Can you come and make a cappuccino? I've got a movie star here and he's being difficult.'

Only then, for the first time, did a little smile cross his lips. In Australia, everyone's a comedian and everyone's equal, and that's the way it should be.

We're not bad at understatement

If a meal or a hotel or a holiday is a dead-set knockout, Australians will describe it as 'not bad'. And, in the same spirit, one of the highest compliments you can give someone is to say, 'You're all right.' It's a type of understatement that's probably always been with us, and probably goes back to our suspicious nature as convicts.

An example. My grandchildren gave my youngest son, Chance, a coffee mug at Christmas. On the side of the mug it said, 'World's Okayest Uncle'. You don't want to go over the top, do you? To be the world's okayest uncle means you are not so bad. You're all right.

In the same way, if the wife's done up for a big night out, and you want to throw her a compliment, you might say, 'You brush up quite nice.' It's a very Australian thing. If you say to your wife, 'You look absolutely lovely, don't change a thing,' and she was brought up Down Under, she's probably going to think, *Okay, what's going on here?* We are wary of flatterers; if people are nice to you, they're after something.

Understatement works in the other direction too. When our team loses due to a blatantly unfair ref's decision, or our dog dies, we don't go, 'That's an outrage!' or 'That's a tragedy.' We say it's 'a bit ordinary'.

If the wife's done up for a big night out, and you want to throw her a compliment, you might say, 'You brush up quite nice.' It's a very Australian thing.

TRADIES RULE!

Another thing I love about Australia is the way tradies are respected. What a great thing that is. In places like England and America, people in the trades are considered second-class citizens. Americans have this obsession with going to college, even though you're only going to get a job at McDonald's at the end of it. In much of the world, if you don't go to university or college, and aren't upper crust or upper caste, it's thought that you're never going to amount to anything.

In Australia, good electricians and plumbers and other tradies of all persuasions can afford their own homes and overseas holidays and lots of the nice life. That's the egalitarian thing. Our tradies are highly respected and not looked down upon – probably because they have such big boats. But it's fair enough that they get the toys. We all know that getting hold of a good plumber or a good electrician is far more important than finding a good philosopher.

And if something *really* dreadful happens, we pull out the great Australian saying 'It could be worse.' In the first big Omicron surge of Covid, when the death toll here was bigger than at the start of the pandemic and we were all locked down pretty tight, I found myself sitting around reading the *Sydney Morning Herald*, looking at all the stories from around the world, and thinking to myself, *It could be worse.* We were better off than the people in Tonga with the tsunami, or in Tornado Alley, where they were getting their houses blown away, or the unfortunate people who were being flooded, or those being jammed into refugee camps.

We do tend to look at things that way, which is pretty good. I've been hearing 'It could be worse' all my life, no matter what happens, no matter how bad it is. Yeah, you fell off the building and broke eleven bones. But you know what? It could have been thirteen. You could be dead. So buck up. It could be worse.

How to Speak 'STRAYAN

she'll be right

Not just a great Australian expression, but a state of mind. It's about Australia's laid-back optimism. 'Yeah, it should be all okay. Everything'll work out fine.' *She'll be right* sums up a very Australian attitude. Like *no worries*.

We prefer to live and let live

Sydney's Mardi Gras started in 1978 and quickly went from a rowdy protest to a TV event and a party that much of Sydney wanted to join. People flew from around the world to take part.

When I was a teenager, even when I was a young man, I heard people all around talking openly about 'pooftas'. Yet none of us – as far as we knew – had ever actually met a real homosexual. They were just some sort of exotic species you made jokes about. We'd never heard of lesbians either. What were they? Did they come from Lebanon?

There were certainly no openly gay people working at the foundry or on the roadworks, or in construction or on the Harbour Bridge. There was no one even suspected of it, though of course, looking back, they would never have been able to admit it. They would have stayed in the closet.

Dykes on Bikes roaring through Sydney streets at the 2020 Mardi Gras. It was one of Sydney's last big parties before the pandemic hit.

When I was still trying to make something of myself in the boxing game, there was a guy at our gym also named Paul. I didn't like sparring with him because he had the coldest ice-coloured eyes. You could hit him as hard as you liked and it never registered, but when he hit you back, it certainly did. Paul turned pro and won his first ten fights in a row, all by knockout.

Then he turned up one night at the pub at Parramatta, hand in hand with another guy. For anyone else, it might have been pretty brave to walk into a working-class pub like that in the 1960s. But what was anyone going to say to a guy who'd just won ten fights by knockout?

I was completely shocked. *He can't be gay*, I thought. *If you're gay you're supposed to flounce around like a sissy. You're not supposed to punch people's heads in.*

When I moved from the blue-collar world into television, I found gay people everywhere. 'So that's where they've been hiding them,' I thought.

When I moved from the blue-collar world into television, I found gay people everywhere. *So that's where they've been hiding them*, I thought. I later realised that the entertainment industry was just where they were accepted and comfortable enough to come out. Our line producer was James 'Jimmy' Fishburn. He was also the choreographer for Les Girls, the famous drag show at Kings Cross, and he'd split his time between that and doing our show. Jimmy and his partner, Nonny, who was an airline steward, were the first openly gay people that I came to know well, and it was a hell of an introduction because you couldn't get anyone more flamboyantly gay than Jimmy. He was a lovely guy and hilarious, and great at his job, which he described as 'being in charge of tits and feathers'. He was also useful in unexpected ways. When we were filming something in the US in the 1970s, we needed to get onto the Universal lot, but there was a complete block on access. Jimmy said, 'Leave that to me.' He made various phone calls during which the words *hello, darling* and *fabulous* were used often and gushingly. Then he turned to us and said, 'Okay, we're filming at Universal tomorrow.' There was a strong gay network in show business and Jimmy was well tapped into it. Alas, there was a tragedy on the way: Jimmy would die of AIDS in 1989.

A lot of comic material from the 1970s and 1980s is going to be looked at differently because of the openness, and I guess wokeness, of everyone today. I wince a bit at some of the skits I made, but at least I know they were all done with an absence of malice. We never meant to hurt or embarrass anybody.

I did a sketch with Arthur Dunger, my character with the potbelly, based on a diehard cricket fan. 'Arfa' was sitting on the hill with his esky, watching the game, when he nodded off and had a nightmare, based on *The Planet of the Apes*. When he woke up, or dreamt he'd woken up, the world had turned into *The Planet of the Poofs*. The gay members of the crew found it hilarious, and, being young and silly, I didn't know any better. I certainly wouldn't do that now. Another skit had two guys wrestling and complimenting each other on their outfits.

Disney wanted to remaster and re-release the first *Dundee* film theatrically in Australia as the coronavirus tailed off. I said the first thing we'd have to do was cut out that scene where Mick goes into the pub and realises the girl he is talking to isn't a girl and then grabs them by the crotch to confirm it. I told Disney the scene had been done in such a different world: it was filmed in 1985, and Mick's ideas dated from the 1950s. We've almost all changed since then, me included, and I understand now why the scene might be considered insulting to transgender people, or even homophobic. In the character's defence, there was no *Les Girls* in Walkabout Creek, where he was raised and lived, and if there was anyone gay in the town, they'd have kept it under wraps. But I could also see it from another perspective now, and understand how it would upset people. 'No, don't re-release it,' I said. 'It's made its mark. I have no interest in doing a director's cut.'

Attitudes have changed and almost all for the good. I've always said there's no point getting 95 percent of people laughing if the rest are crying in the corner. I don't want to hurt or shame anyone. Except maybe a few people in the Australian Tax Office, but that's another matter.

Same-sex marriage and LGBTQI rights were rearing their heads in Australia long before many other Western countries, even if things like marriage equality didn't get put into law until a bit later because the politicians were lagging behind the people. I'm so pleased we've become so much more accepting in so many ways, delighted that we've moved so far forward.

Attitudes have changed and almost all for the good. I've always said there's no point getting 95 percent of people laughing if the rest are crying in the corner.

We're working on bringing everyone together

In late November 2021, my mate David Gulpilil returned to the Dreamtime. Gulli had been fighting a really aggressive cancer for four years and no one was shocked when he died. In fact, everyone was amazed he had lasted that long. But his death was a sad loss in our history and to our culture.

He was probably the most famous Original Australian, certainly of our time, maybe of all time. This Yolngu man was known and recognised around the world for his ability to act and tell stories in dance and music. He won over everyday Australians to the point where he became a symbol of the culture that we so nearly lost.

And what a life. Gulli was born in 1953, so for the first fourteen years of his life, he wasn't even counted as part of the Australian population. It's shocking that, for more than 150 years, the Originals were not thought of as real citizens. At least the 1967 referendum brought an overwhelming yes vote: 90.77 percent of Australians wanted the change.

Gulli spoke several Aboriginal languages as well as English. In 1971 the film I mentioned earlier, *Walkabout*, made him famous (though I think it's more correct to say he made the film *Walkabout* famous) and he toured the world and was introduced to such people as John Lennon, Bob Marley and Marlon Brando. Yet back home his people still weren't being treated with the respect they deserved.

By the time he died, there had been a big rethink about the timing of Australia Day. The Aboriginal flag – once banned in many situations – was flying almost everywhere, including

One of the greatest Australians: dancer, actor, storyteller (in several languages) and all-round good bloke, the late, great and much-missed David 'Gulli' Gulpilil.

on top of the Sydney Harbour Bridge, Prime Minister Kevin Rudd had apologised to the Stolen Generations, and Welcome to Country and Acknowledgement of Country ceremonies had become commonplace. There's still a long way to go, but there's a lot of goodwill, and most blow-ins – a term that includes anyone who arrived in 1788 or afterwards – are finally acknowledging that this was someone else's place first.

We stick tight and believe in the fair go

Everyone sort of looked down on our former prime minister 'Little Johnny' Howard, or so it seemed, though he kept winning elections. And whatever you think of his politics, he deserves respect because he did what the Americans have failed to do: he got rid of most of the guns. He is much admired in the States as a result, at least among those with common sense.

Howard didn't worry about the reaction from the hardliners and other conservatives from his own side of politics. He just said people had been shooting each other and we couldn't have that. It was a direct reaction to the horrible events at Port Arthur in Tasmania in 1996, when a rogue gunman murdered thirty-five people.

The rest of Australia had a lot of guns too, of course, and this wasn't an isolated incident. Twelve years earlier, when I was just about to fly to the US to film the 'shrimp on the barbie' tourism commercials, there was an armed battle between Sydney bikies in a pub car park, which became known as the Milperra Massacre. It made headlines around the world, particularly since a fourteen-year-old girl was killed in the crossfire. I remember thinking, *Oh Jesus, that's just awful. That poor girl. And a tragedy like that's not going to help us attract anyone to our country.*

Anyway, after Port Arthur, John Howard stared down our own US-style noisy gun nuts and said, 'Enough is enough.' And the average Australian, to his and her everlasting credit, said, 'Yeah. Okay. Fair enough.' They didn't go out and attack parliament, or try to kill their leaders, the way they would in the US if anyone tried to take away their guns.

Whatever people think of the former prime minister John Howard, most admire the way he stood up in front of pro-gun protesters and told them why they couldn't have US-style access to firearms. Howard was wearing a bulletproof vest, and if you'd seen the crowd, you'd have worn one too.

So how did we end up mixing a convict-born suspicion of authority with such obedience? It sounds like a contradiction, but I don't think it is. Sure, we've become incredibly law-abiding. We gave up our guns, the vast majority of us followed all the Covid rules, and we went and got vaccinated. You'd think we'd be the exact opposite, that we would still be telling authority to go to buggery.

But no, and I think it's all to do with the egalitarian thing. We don't like the boofheads running the country, most of the time, so our compliance is less about obeying them than sticking together. You know, 'I'm not doing it for him, the man, I'm doing it for my friends and neighbours.' We say, 'Okay, it's a fair thing. I'll get vaccinated because I don't want to go and kill your grandmother. She's a lovely old lady, and I see her every week when I mow the lawn.'

We're not jumping in line because our fearless leader said to, we're doing it out of respect for others. We're obedient because we believe in a fair go. I think that's why the gun thing worked. Australians didn't say, 'You're taking away our guns. That breaches our right to freedom. You're never going to get them, except from my cold, dead hands.' They instead said, 'A lot of people have been killed, so, yeah, fair enough.'

We help each other

A lot about Australia hasn't changed. Here's one of my favourite examples. If you're in a back street somewhere and your car breaks down, stick the bonnet up and stand alongside it and look hopeless. Someone will always pull up, particularly once you start getting out of the city a bit. Yep, some boofhead will get out, heave up his shoulders and say confidently, 'Go on, gi's a look.' Even if you're an ugly bloke, you won't be standing there for hours like you would in many other countries. That's something I've always been proud of.

I must admit I was never too great mechanically, so I'd tend to pull over only if it was a good sort in distress. Then I'd stick my melon under the bonnet, wiggle a few wires and hoses, and hope to God it started. But most of the time, guys who pulled up really did know what they were doing. It was in our nature, our makeup, especially among us working-class folks. We couldn't afford professional mechanics.

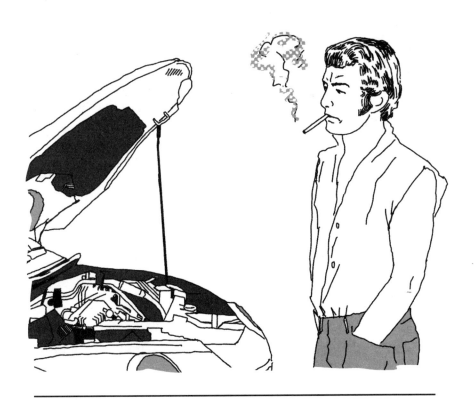

We're getting there

No matter who you are or what country you live in, you always whinge about the place, talk about what's wrong and how the place is being badly managed and so on. But I'm one of those fortunate people who's been to a lot of different countries, and whenever I return to Oz, the penny drops as to how lucky we are.

Australia is inarguably the youngest, most progressive, most rapidly developed place in history. We have a civilised independent government. We have an army, navy and air force, and education and health systems we can be proud of.

We're more advanced in many ways than some countries that have been around for thousands of years. We've gone from a hodgepodge collection of disreputables in a prison farm to a proper nation in about three lifetimes, and we were one of the founding members of the United Nations.

You can come here from China, Mexico, the Middle East, anywhere in the world, and if you want to live here and enjoy our style of life, then you're going to be quickly accepted. That's why, from what I've seen, this is pretty much the most cosmopolitan, mixed-up-from-everywhere place on earth. There are 27 million of us, most of us come from somewhere else, and yet we're getting on pretty damn well.

I reckon it's our greatest achievement. As I said earlier, we're not perfect – I'm not pretending that – but we are most certainly working on it.

'I STILL CALL AUSTRALIA ...'

When I was a kid, we sang 'God Save the Queen', even though she didn't really need saving. She was doing just fine.

As our population became more diverse, it was a bit much to ask New Australians to be singing 'God Save the Queen'. There was no reason Italians and Greeks and Arabs would think of her as their queen.

That's why, in 1984, we finally adopted our own anthem, 'Advance Australia Fair'. It was a good choice, partly because it has that important word *fair* in the title, though it has some weird-arse words in it too, including *girt*.

We haven't got rid of *girt* yet, but we did change 'Australia's sons let us rejoice' to 'Australians all let us rejoice'. And it dawned on us that we weren't 'young and free', not with some of us having been here for 60,000 years or so. So now it's 'Australians all let us rejoice, for we are one and free'. It's not poetry, but it fits.

It was my mate Allan Johnson of Mojo who wrote the sporting anthem that at one stage you heard played more than you heard the national anthem: 'C'mon Aussie, C'mon.' He was an advertising genius.

My own personal anthem is 'I Still Call Australia Home' by Peter Allen. For most Aussies who travel a lot, or spend some extended time in another country, that's their song too. I got into trouble with a lot of people when I was pouring crap on 'Waltzing Matilda', which some still think should be our national anthem. But what a silly song it is. An unbalanced swagman does stupid things, and his sheep is grinning too, so the sheep is obviously stupid as well. Give me 'I Still Call Australia Home' any day.

ABOUT
PAUL HOGAN

Paul Hogan AM was a rigger on the Sydney Harbour Bridge before rising to fame in the early 1970s with his own comedy sketch program, *The Paul Hogan Show*. The series ran for more than a decade, and was popular both in Australia and around the world, introducing hilarious characters such as Leo Wanker, Arthur Dunger and Luigi the Unbelievable. In 1985, Hogan was chosen as Australian of the Year and was inducted into the Order of Australia. In 1986 he starred in his first movie, *Crocodile Dundee*. It went on to become the most successful independent movie ever, earning him a Golden Globe Award for Best Actor in a Comedy and an Academy Award nomination for Best Original Screenplay, and making him a household name worldwide. Following the success of *Crocodile Dundee*, Hogan hosted the Academy Awards and starred in several other films, including *Crocodile Dundee II*, *Almost an Angel*, *Lightning Jack*, *Charlie & Boots* and *The Very Excellent Mr Dundee*.

Acknowledgements

I'd like to thank my great mate and tormentor, Dean Murphy, for yet again forcing me off the couch, sticking a pencil in my hand and shouting 'Get to work!' I'd also like to thank Tony Davis for once again taking my scribbles, musings and half thoughts and helping us knock them into a shape so good that my schoolteachers would be proud.

I must thank Jude McGee and the whole team at HarperCollins. This is our second book together and, who knows, if I live to be a hundred there might be a third called something like *Now Where Was I?*

Finally, I need to thank my entire family, but particularly those who feature in the early parts of this book. With the help of a judge or two from the Old Bailey, they made the long journey to Oz and, in doing so, set us up as one of the luckiest families in the world.

Picture Credits

Illustrations by Pilar Costabal, unless indicated otherwise.

NOTE: While all efforts have been made to trace and acknowledge all copyright holders, in some cases these may have been unsuccessful. If you believe you hold copyright in an image, please contact the publisher.

INTRODUCTION

Paul Hogan as a toddler, courtesy Paul Hogan

Ron Clarke lighting the Olympic Torch, 1956, Getty Images

Paul Hogan on the Sydney Harbour Bridge, courtesy Paul Hogan

CHAPTER 1

Waddy (detail), Wikimedia Commons

Boomerang (detail), Ian Dagnall / Alamy Stock Photo

Emu, iStock

Dingo, Torpy / Shutterstock

Tasmanian devil, Bernhard Richter / Shutterstock

Frill-necked lizard, Ken Griffiths / Shutterstock

Funnel-web spider, Paul Looyen / Shutterstock

Willem Janszoon, 17th century, BNA Photographic / Alamy Stock Photo

Anthony Van Diemen, c. 1709–1737, Wikimedia Commons

Galah, iStock

Notice issued to quell the gold miners' rebellion in Ballarat, Victoria, 1854, Lakeview Images / Alamy Stock Photo

The Queen and the Duke of Edinburgh on the Royal train as it leaves Bathurst, NSW, 1954, PA Images / Getty Images

Wild boar, The Jungle Explorer / Shutterstock

Cane toad, Johan Larson / Shutterstock

Niagara Café, Gundagai, c. 1940

Peter Bol after competing in the men's 800 m semi-final at the Tokyo Olympic Games in 2021, Abbie Parr / Getty Images

CHAPTER 2

Charles Laughton, still from Mutiny on the Bounty, Alamy Stock Photo

The Arrest of Governor Bligh, 1808, Wikimedia Commons

Social Purity Society, c. 1883, SA History Hub / Wikimedia Commons

Helen Reddy, 1973, Wikimedia Commons

On the set of Anzacs with Andrew Clarke, courtesy Paul Hogan

Vegemite advertisement, 1940

Furphys, Shepparton, 1905, Alamy Stock Photo

Harbour Bridge Riggers, 1930–1932, by Ted Hood, State Library of NSW

Paul Hogan on Sydney Harbour Bridge, 1976, Sydney Morning Herald / Getty Images

Advertisement on the occasion of the American naval squadron visiting Brisbane, 1941, State Library of Queensland

Jack Hogan, courtesy Paul Hogan

Victory celebrations in Sydney, 1945, State Library of Victoria

CHAPTER 3

Australian cricket tour of England team, 1882, Alamy Stock Photo

The Ashes urn, Alamy Stock Photo

Model of R.B. Smith's 1876 stump-jump plough, Museums Victoria

Australian tennis fans at the Australian Open, 2016, Leonard Zhukovsky / Shutterstock

Mallee bull statue in Birchip, Victoria, birchip.vic.au

Graham 'Polly' Farmer, Getty Images

Bob Hawke, America's Cup win, 1983, The Age, Getty Images

Watching TV at Coles, Hay Street, Perth, 1960, Coles Myer / State Library of Victoria

Paul Hogan parades during the 2000 Sydney Olympic Games closing ceremony, Robert Cianflone / Getty Images

Snowy Baker, Duke Kahanamoku and Frank Beaurepaire, State Library of NSW

Don Bradman at the wicket at practice, 1932, by Sam Hood, State Library of NSW

Cathy Freeman after winning gold in the 400 m final at the Sydney Olympic Games, 2000, Nick Wilson / Getty Images

Johnny Devitt after winning gold in the 100 m final at the Rome Olympic Games, 1960, Wikimedia Commons

Lionel Rose, 1969, by Val Hopwood, Wikimedia Commons

Ash Barty in the women's quarter-final at the Australian Open, 2022, Mark Metcalfe / Getty Images

Steven Bradbury after winning gold in the men's speed-skating final at the Salt Lake City Winter Olympic Games, 2002, Mike Hewitt / Getty Images

CHAPTER 4

AC/DC in London, 1976, Michael Putland / Getty Images

The Black Stump Hotel in Merriwagga, NSW, courtesy Sharon Stuart

William Buckley, 1857, print from engraving by Frederick Grosse, State Library of Victoria

Crocodile hunter Steve Irwin, Paul Smith / Shutterstock

The Myer Emporium, Melbourne, 1934, by Herbert, Harold B. (Harold Brocklebank), State Library of Victoria

Mixed-breed dog, sixpixx / Shutterstock

Ozzie the Mozzie at Hexham Bowling Club, NSW, Stuart Edwards / Wikimedia Commons

Phar Lap in the Melbourne Museum, Wikimedia Commons

Reg Grundy, publicity still for *Reg Grundy's Wheel of Fortune*

Riggers enjoy smoko high up above Sydney harbour beside a creeper crane cabin, Ted Hood / Alamy Stock Photo

Road train driver with her truck at the Nullarbor Roadhouse, SA, Rob Walls / Alamy Stock Photo

CHAPTER 5

Home made at the Vandyke factory in Villawood, NSW, 1949, State Library of NSW

Window display of a WashMaster wringer washing machine at Marcus Clark's, 1939, State Library of NSW

Backyard dunny, Suzanne-B / Shutterstock

Clay, Brett and Todd, courtesy Paul Hogan

Feeding the milk-cart horse, 1951, R. Donaldson, State Library of NSW

Prime Minister Ben Chifley at the launch of the Holden FX, 1948, National Archives of Australia

King Henry VIII, Alamy Stock Photo

Paul, Wendy and Pat Hogan, courtesy Paul Hogan

First Communion, courtesy Paul Hogan

Johnny O'Keefe with Radio 4TO announcer Stewart 'Stuie' McInnes, 1969, Wikimedia Commons

The Wild One handout, 1953, Columbia TriStar / Getty Images

Paul Hogan having a drink in a pub in Paddington, NSW, John Carnemolla / Corbis via Getty Images

Ladies lounge at the Tallangatta Hotel, Victoria, 1954, State Library of Victoria

Joe Bugner before his fight with Joe Frazier, London, 1973, *Evening Standard* / Hulton Archive / Getty Images

Unknown newlyweds, c. 1950, State Library of NSW

Dinner time, temporary home, Townsville, Queensland, 1940–1945, State Library of Victoria

Dinki Di Dogs Eyes pie shop, Dunedoo, NSW, chris24 / Alamy Stock Photo

Gold-plated Chiko Roll at the Museum of the Riverina, Wagga Wagga, NSW, 2008, Wikimedia Commons

Anna Pavlova, 1905, Wikimedia Commons

Lamingtons, Milleflore Images / Shutterstock

CHAPTER 6

Bondi in march-past, SLSA premiers, c. 1935, State Library of NSW

Lifesaver, St Kilda Life Saving Club, Surf Life Saving, sls.com.au

Duke Kahanamoku surfing tandem with Viola Hartman, Corona del Mar, 1922, MediaNews Group / Orange County Register via Getty Images

Surf lifesavers at Era Beach, Royal National Park, NSW

Strop (John Cornell) and Paul Hogan, publicity still for *The Paul Hogan Show*

Adelaide City Baths, 1950, State Records of SA

Kiandra Snow Shoe Club, 1900, Wikimedia Commons

Mr Allan Scott, Bookmaker at Rosehill Racecourse, 1973, Fairfax Media Archive / Getty Images

Greyhound, David Jar / Shutterstock

Paul Hogan courtesy Paul Hogan

The Wild One – Marlon Brando with Peggy Maley and Yvonne Doughty, 1953, Photo 12 / Alamy Stock Photo

Darwin Stubbies, Wikimedia Commons

Roxy Theatre, Parramatta, NSW

Jenny Agutter and David Gulpilil, *Walkabout*, 1971, Everett Collection Inc. / Alamy Stock Photo

Mel Gibson in *Mad Max*, 1979, Everett Collection Inc. / Alamy Stock Photo

James Cromwell and Magda Szubanski, *Babe: Pig in the City*, 1998, Allstar Picture Library Ltd / Alamy Stock Photo

Anthony Simcoe, Anne Tenney, Michael Caton, Sophie Lee, Eric Bana, Wayne Hope and Stephen Curry in *The Castle*, 1997, Everett Collection Inc. / Alamy Stock Photo

CHAPTER 7

Samuel Marsden, 1764–1838, c. 1913, Wikimedia Commons

Ned Kelly, 1880, State Library of Victoria

Errol Flynn in *The Adventures of Robin Hood*, 1938, Entertainment Pictures / Alamy Stock Photo

Granville Cinema, 1942, State Library of NSW

Johnny Sattler on the shoulders of teammates after winning the rugby league grand final, 1971, John O'Gready, *Sydney Morning Herald* / Publishing Nine

Captain Peter Janson, 2009, Justin McManus, *The Age* / Publishing Nine

Before a Bachelors and Spinsters Ball, Ariah Park, NSW, 2016, Peter Parks / Getty Images

The departure of the Burke and Wills expedition in 1860, 1881, J.D. A.H. Massina & Co., State Library of Victoria

Dawn Fraser at the Rome Olympic Games, 1960, Wikimedia Commons

Germaine Greer, 1969, Estate of Keith Morris / Getty Images

Australian Test Cricketer David Boon, Rob Walls / Alamy Stock Photo

Gough Whitlam watches Bob Hawke drink beer from a yard glass, 1972, News Ltd / Newspix

Paul Hogan, John Cornell as Strop, and Delvene Delaney, publicity shot for *The Paul Hogan Show*

John Cornell, 1986, Ross Willis / *Sydney Morning Herald* / Publishing Nine

Paul Hogan, Delvene Delaney and John Cornell

CHAPTER 8

CWA rooms and Marathon Café, Weethalle, 2011, Wikimedia Commons

Mardi Gras parade, Sydney, NSW, 2020, Fimina Anna / Shutterstock

David Gulpilil at Sydney Film Festival Opening Night, 2006, Patrick Riviere / Getty Images

Prime Minister John Howard at a pro-gun rally in Sale, Victoria, 1996, Ray Strange / Newspix

HarperCollinsPublishers
Australia • Brazil • Canada • France • Germany • Holland • India
Italy • Japan • Mexico • New Zealand • Poland • Spain • Sweden
Switzerland • United Kingdom • United States of America

HarperCollins acknowledges the Traditional Custodians
of the land upon which we live and work, and pays respect
to Elders past and present.

First published in Australia in 2022
by HarperCollinsPublishers Australia Pty Limited
Gadigal Country
Level 13, 201 Elizabeth Street, Sydney NSW 2000
ABN 36 009 913 517
harpercollins.com.au

A catalogue record for this book is available from the National Library of Australia

ISBN 978 1 4607 6229 5 (paperback)
ISBN 978 1 4607 1505 5 (ebook)

Cover and internal design by Lisa Reidy
Illustrations by Pilar Costabal
Cover images: photo of the author courtesy Paul Hogan; Sydney Harbour Bridge by
4FR / iStock; back cover by Paul Murray / *Sydney Morning Herald*
Typeset in Garamond Pro by Lisa Reidy
Printed and bound in Australia by McPherson's Printing Group